General Gordon

General Gordon

Richard Garrett

ARTHUR BARKER LIMITED LONDON
A subsidiary of Weidenfeld (Publishers) Limited

Printed in Great Britain by
Bristol Typesetting Company Limited
Barton Manor, St Philips
Bristol

Contents

Illustrations

Gordon in the trenches before Sebastopol, 1855 *(Mansell Collection)*

Storming Soochow, November 1863 *(Radio Times Hulton Picture Library)*

Gordon in Chinese costume *(Mansell Collection)*

The house which Gordon occupied at Gravesend *(Radio Times)*

Teaching the 'wangs' at Gravesend 1867 *(Radio Times)*

Gordon leaving Charing Cross on his last mission to the Sudan, 1884 *(Radio Times)*

Khartoum as it was during the siege *(Mansell Collection)*

Gordon's last stand *(Mansell Collection)*

A contemporary cartoon depicting Gladstone's failure to save Gordon *(Mary Evans Picture Library)*

Gordon's head is brought to Slatin Pasha *(Mary Evans)*

The Governor-General of Khartoum as he will be remembered *(Mansell Collection)*

The author and publisher would like to thank the Mansell Collection, the Radio Times Hulton Picture Library and the Mary Evans Picture Library for the kind permission to reproduce the above illustrations.

Maps

On pages 233 and 234

China: Shanghai and environs
Egypt and the Sudan

Acknowledgements

The author would like to thank the librarians of the London Library, The Royal Engineers' Institution at Chatham, and the National Maritime Museum for their invaluable help; also the multitude of writers who have produced books about General Gordon, the back numbers of *The Times*, the *Illustrated London News*, and the *Pall Mall Gazette* (which prove so conclusively Lord Macaulay's assertion that 'the only true history of a country is to be found in its newspapers'). My thanks also to Mrs Susan Reid, who typed the manuscript and managed to make sense out of what must have been a bewildering scrawl of revisions.

Early One Morning

The shooting started at about 3.30 a.m. General Gordon, who had been sleeping uneasily and was not feeling well, got up. He put on a dressing-gown, lit a cigarette, and climbed the staircase leading to the palace roof. It was pitch dark outside. The quarter moon had set at one o'clock. Now only a scattering of stars pierced the dense black night.

He walked to the edge of the roof. There were few lights to indicate what was happening, and communications with the forward troops seemed to have broken down. Most of the fire appeared to be coming from the west gate of the city. In a rising babble, the high-pitched cries of the attackers suggested that they were meeting with some success. It was hardly surprising. His own troops were tired, underfed and demoralized. It was, he reflected bitterly, a very different body of men from that of a few months earlier. Then he had been hailed as the saviour of Khartoum; but the long months of the siege had eroded this confidence. Now, nobody believed that a victory was possible. The native soldiers fought because there was no alternative. It was better to be killed by a bullet than to suffer the Mahdi's tortures.

Gordon called an orderly over to him. He told him to send a message to the engineer of the steamer *Ismailia*. He was to raise steam as quickly as possible. The man was also to bring back a crew to operate the gun on the palace roof. He looked again in the direction of the firing, but it was still too dark to see anything.

Some while later, the dishevelled runner reported that the *Ismailia*'s engineer was not on board the ship. He was, it seemed, too frightened to leave his house. The fighting was still some way away: for the time being, there was nothing more to be done.

He went downstairs to his dressing-room. He put on a white uniform, his sword, and he picked up a revolver. The time had passed quickly: it was now about five o'clock, and a pale splash of light was spreading across the sky from the east. The noises of battle were much louder: there seemed to be fewer shots, and an increasing tumult of shrieks. Like a storm of sound, the victory cries of the Dervishes seemed to envelop the palace. The resistance of his own men had ceased. Even the gun on the palace roof was silent – presumably because it could not be depressed sufficiently to fire on the enemy. They were too close.

Amid this insane hubbub, he was a small and isolated figure of tranquillity. Taking his time, he walked to the top of the stairs which led to the palace council chamber. There was a throng of Dervishes at the foot of them: four men, braver than the rest, were coming up towards him. The leading figure, a warrior named Shahin, was waving his spear in a gesture of fury. Gordon made a small shrug of defiance, before Shahin's spear hit him. He spun round, and a second spear embedded itself in his back. He fell forward on to his face. The three other warriors, all of them veterans of the Mahdi's earliest campaigns, attacked him with their swords, but that second thrust from the spear had already killed him. General Charles George Gordon, Governor-General of the Sudan, was dead. The shrieks of the mob became even louder. The sun hoisted itself into the sky. It was five-thirty in the morning of 26 January 1885.

PART I

The Soldier

1

The Days of Youth

Born on 28 January 1833, at 1 Kemp Terrace, Woolwich Common, to Elizabeth (née Enderby) and Henry William Gordon, a son (Charles George).

A quick glance at an almanac will show that the birth date of 28 January put the new baby under the sign of Aquarius. He would, the astrologers suggest, be sympathetic, unobtrusive, impetuous, tenacious – to mention but a few of the characteristics. According to one distinguished seer,* the knowledge and power of Aquarians are 'poured out from on high for the good of mankind'. That, one might say, is an ambitious specification; but let us see, Aquarius, how this child, who arrived at a time which has not been recorded, and at a place which overlooks the greensward of the common, matches up to it.

His character will, of course, require time before it is formed. It will slip, like a collection of lantern slides, from one phase to the next, until it sets in a distinguishable pattern. Eventually, we shall have an almost complete portrait of the man who died at Khartoum two days before his fifty-third birthday. Even so, despite his letters and journals, despite the recollections of those who knew him, despite the works of all the other biographers, we shall never completely discover the truth. Often it seems as if two men died within the body of Gordon, early that day in the Sudanese capital. There was a soldier, and there may have been a saint. Whilst the two did not live wholly separate lives, the one went about his business with little interference from the other.

* Maurice Woodruff.

Professionally, Charles George Gordon was a soldier: it was, perhaps, a family tradition. His great grandfather, David Gordon, served in the 47th Regiment during the '45 Rebellion. He was taken prisoner by Prince Charles's troops at the battle of Prestonpans. Afterwards, he was paroled by his captors. When the war was over, he emigrated to Canada, where he died at Halifax, Nova Scotia.

His son was named William Augustus after the Duke of Cumberland, who was one of his godfathers. William Gordon, too, was a military man. He was present at the siege of Louisberg in the Seven Years War, and fought under Wolfe at the capture of Quebec. He married the sister of the vicar of Hexham in Norfolk: the couple had three sons and four daughters. Their youngest was a lad named Henry William. The other boys died young, but Henry William grew to manhood and joined the Royal Artillery in 1803.

The previous Gordons appear as unsubstantial characters: shadows which appear briefly in the background, and tell us little. Henry William is more clearly defined. He was born in Devonshire and, even though he came from a Highland family, he always liked to think of himself as a Devonian. He was obviously a good soldier, for he became a lieutenant-general. Most accounts suggest that he was a strict disciplinarian, though this is difficult to believe. When his children were young, he does not seem to have exercised the iron control that was (or was supposed to be) the mark of a Victorian parent. He was certainly blessed with a sense of humour; and, no doubt because he had a large family to support, he was a thrifty man. He encouraged the young Gordons to be likewise.

If Henry William Gordon produced the soldier in his son Charles's make-up, his wife must have been responsible for the saint. Elizabeth Enderby's family were pious people, who operated a fleet of whaling ships from bases in London and New England. They may have, figuratively, carried a harpoon in one hand: they certainly held a Bible in the other. In their search for new hunting grounds, they became important sponsors of nineteenth-century polar exploration. They are also said to have been the first company to send ships to the west coast of America by way of Cape Horn. Charles Enderby founded the London Geographical Society. His brother, Sam, was the father of Elizabeth. From him, she inherited the belief that the Bible was the only book worth reading – and that it should be read again and again. We see her as a pleasant, capable woman: devoted to her large family, and secure in her faith that what will be will be – and, if in any doubt, look it up in the Good Book. The answers, as she frequently told her children, were all there.

Henry William Gordon and Elizabeth Enderby were married in 1817. They produced eleven children, of whom Charles George was the fourth. Of his brothers and sisters, Augusta (twelve years his senior) and Henry were the most important to him. Henry, loyal and understanding, was the recipient of the soldier's confidences. Augusta, prim, possessive, and pious beyond belief, received the outpourings of the saint. With such a large tribe to look after, Mrs Gordon was in the habit of delegating responsibility to the able Augusta. She certainly did not take the place of his mother, who was devoted to him ('Oh! How she loved me,' he once wrote); but, nevertheless, her role in his life transcended that of a sister. Above all things, probably, she was a buttress against doubt.

Of his three brothers, Enderby (the eldest) and Henry both became soldiers. Freddy, the youngest, was delicate: he died before he had any opportunity to make his mark in the world.

The Gordon family – multiplying, one might say, as it went – moved from one military station to another. From Woolwich, Henry William was posted to Pidgeon House Fort, Dublin, and thence to the fort at Leith. Young Charles was said to have disliked the bangs of the garrison's guns, which was hardly surprising in an infant of his age. He is supposed to have manfully concealed his fears, which sounds like a desperate attempt to extend the hero's reputation to the child. Later, when his father was put in charge of the gunners at Corfu, a budding fearlessness was attributed to what, when all is said and done, was a rather silly and tiresome prank.

He used to throw himself off a rock into deep water, knowing that he was unable to swim. Somebody had to dive in and rescue him. Since nine-year-olds, even when they are such potentially complex characters as this child, are not usually suffering from a death wish, we have to assume that he was merely trying to draw attention to himself. However, his room at the hotel was next to that of the Duke of Cambridge, who appears to have liked the lad in spite of the strain he must have put upon the patience of his officers.

At the age of ten, Charles returned to England, where he was sent to boarding school at Taunton. The choice of establishment was made, simply, because the headmaster was the brother of one of the innumerable governesses who had tutored the wandering Gordons. The boy is said to have been indifferent at games; good at mapmaking and drawing. Later, he attended a place in Shooter's Hill, S.E. London, where he was coached for admission to the Royal Military Academy at Woolwich.

By this time, the rest of the family had moved back to England, and his father had taken up the post of director of the carriage department at the Royal Arsenal, Woolwich. Their house was opposite the garrison commander's, which cannot have been to the comfort of Gordon senior. No matter how much of a martinet he may have been to his troops, he was less than a match for the unruly squad of youngsters at home.

The young Gordons were nothing if not high spirited. They smuggled captured mice into the home of the garrison commander. They invented a crossbow (it fired screws), which smashed twenty-seven windows in a single afternoon, and nearly dispatched an unfortunate captain who happened to be passing. On one occasion, they even had the temerity to launch an attack on the Royal Military Academy while a lecture was in progress.

It is hardly surprising that, in a moment of desperation, their father once observed that 'I feel like a man sitting on a powder barrel.' Whether the ultimate eruption would come

16

from the senior officer across the way, or from the family within, was a matter of doubt. Certainly, during this period, young Charles gave no evidence of the piety which was later to govern much of his life. When sister Augusta received her religious tracts by post, it was a matter for jesting. At church on Sundays, while others slumbered through the long sermons, Charles and his brothers and sisters found relief in the fact that, according to Victorian custom, their pew was curtained off. 'You could have made your toilet there,' he recalled in later life, 'and none would have been any the wiser.' Poor Augusta! How she must have frowned upon her younger relatives, as they interrupted her already substantial intake of divine knowledge!

Eventually Charles George Gordon followed his brothers Enderby and Henry into the military academy. He was, true to his father's calling, to go into the gunners.

The Royal Military Academy of those days has been described by E. S. Turner in *Officers and Gentlemen* as 'a species of Hell-on-the-Thames'. It had been founded in 1741 for officer cadets destined for the Royal Artillery and the Royal Engineers – specialist regiments, that is to say, in which commissions could not be bought, and in which promotion could only be obtained from seniority. As originally conceived, the inmates were aged from 14 to 17. When this was raised to 16 to 18, no attempt was made to modify the rules. The cadets were compelled to undress for bed in the dark; they were allowed out for exercise in a small playground, and smoking was punished by forty-eight hours' solitary confinement in a room, six feet by eight feet, in which there was no bed, no light, and no fire. Two pounds was the maximum allowed for six months' pocket money, and the cadets were permitted to change their linen only on three specified days a week.

If the regulations were not enough to make a cadet's life a misery, his companions, in the robustly brutal manner of Victorian education, were only too eager to add to his suffering. Back in 1819, the Duke of Wellington had dismissed eleven of them for bullying – with the result that their fathers had been compelled to buy them commissions in line regiments. But this did little to check the tyranny of the more senior cadets. Newcomers to the academy were roasted over an open fire in their nightshirts. They were thrown naked through an open window. Or, they were compelled to bend over with their hand on the ground, and their bodies at an angle of forty-five degrees. Their feet were then kicked away from under them, and they fell flat and miserably on their faces. Bullying of young officers was commonplace in the army, but *The United Service Magazine* 'thought that these abominable outrages were confined to Woolwich Academy or to such sinks as Harrow and Eton, where the boys of larger growth, as a preparation for their future career, are encouraged to flog and torture their little school fellows'.

When Charles Gordon went there, the commandant was an irascible veteran of the Napoleonic Wars, named General Parker, who had lost a leg at Waterloo. He, too, has been given credit for comparing young Gordon to 'a barrel of gunpowder', though this seems unlikely. The general was well able to look after himself. On the other hand, if he was an immovable force, Cadet Gordon was not far from being an irresistible object. Some years earlier, the Gordon family had been promised a visit to Astleys Circus as a treat. Young Charles had been accused of some misdeed or other, and had been told that he would not be allowed to accompany the rest of them. This rankled. He protested his innocence, and told anyone who was prepared to listen that he was being unjustly punished. Eventually, it was conceded that his guilt had not been fairly established. The embargo was withdrawn, and he was told that he might attend the show after all. But Charles was not content with the restoration of his circus-going rights. He had been a victim of injustice: as an act of protest, he now *refused* to go.

At the academy, a similar mulishness made itself evident. On one occasion, an instructor told him that little short of a miracle would be required to make him an officer. Gordon, who had a number of good conduct badges and had been complimented for his work on fortifications and his ability as a surveyor, considered the remark beyond the bounds of reasonable criticism. He immediately ripped off his epaulettes, and hurled them at the officer's feet.

On another occasion, one of the senior cadets had kept the rest of them in the dining-hall for what seemed to be an unnecessarily long time. The hall was approached by a narrow staircase, and the young tyrant was standing at the head of it. Gordon's impatience mounted. He bent over, charged the cadet, caught him in the middle, and sent him spinning down the steps and through the glass doors at the bottom. The crime, which caused him to be stripped of his privileges and confined to his quarters, was the makings of his reputation as 'a wild young man'.

But there was something more serious in store. Gordon has been described as having 'an almost feminine gentleness'. Quite possibly: but he also had a fierce temper, which exploded instantly and usually departed with equal speed. On this occasion, a junior cadet had done, or said, something to annoy him. Gordon erupted and struck him on the head with a clothes brush. It was not, as even his victim admitted, a heavy blow, but it came to the notice of General Parker, who was carrying out one of his periodical assaults on bullying. The outcome was that it cost Charles Gordon six months' seniority. He was, they all said, lucky not to have been dismissed.

Gordon was as ambitious as the next man. This setback would mean that, by the time he eventually got into the gunners, all his contemporaries would be half a year ahead of him – and, due to the corp's insistence on seniority, there would be no way of catching them up. Consequently, he rapidly revised his ideas. He no longer wished to join the Royal Artillery. Indeed, he would try for a commission in the Royal Engineers.

His father must have been disappointed at the news. The gunners were proper soldiers: the sappers were eccentric characters who, according to a catchphrase which survived

for a great many years, were either 'mad, married, or metho-
dist'. Some suggested that they were more civilians than
soldiers, which did them a great deal less than justice. They
brought civilian skills to the profession of arms; but, in an
assault, they were right up in front, clearing the obstacles
away for the infantry.

Gordon duly, if belatedly, passed into the Royal Engineers.
'Those terrible examinations – how I remember them!' he
once told a young relative. 'Sometimes I dream of them.' Still,
he covered himself with sufficient glory, and was gazetted as
a second lieutenant. He was told to report to the corp's headquarters at Chatham. For the next two years, he studied the
more practical aspects of military engineering. His senior
officers found him intelligent and hardworking. His wildness,
for the time being at any rate, seemed to have spent itself. At
the end of this final part of his training, he was posted to
Pembrokeshire on 24 January 1854.

Lieutenant Charles George Gordon was now twenty-one years
of age. He was good looking, with a neatly trimmed moustache
and curly brown hair. His height was five feet nine inches.
He was a wiry, impatient figure, who walked with quick steps
and his head thrust forward. Indoors, he would pace up and
down the room, smoking countless cigarettes, and sometimes
grabbing the arm of his companion to emphasize a point. His
moods varied from a calm dignity which seemed almost
reposeful, to sudden outbreaks of indignation, which were
signalled by his voice. At these moments, the normally soft
cadences were speeded up, and the sound level rose. But the
squall was soon over, and there he was, the words resuming
their almost tender passage from his mouth, and the talk from
time to time interrupted by a quick smile. He was by no means
an erect and military figure, and it was not his bearing which
compelled attention so much as his unusually clear blue eyes.
Everyone who knew him was impressed by them. According
to one admirer, they 'seemed to have magical power over all
who came within [their] influence'. From another: 'their ex-

pression was one of settled feverishness, the colour blue-grey as is the sky on a bitter March morning'. And, from another, 'Gordon's eyes looked you through and through.' Unfortunately for Gordon their efficiency was not equal to their reputation, for he was colour blind.

A depot for the Royal Navy and a large arsenal were under construction at Pembroke, and a system of fortifications had been designed to protect them. It was a busy place, with a thriving shipyard. During Gordon's service there, five vessels were launched, and a new Royal yacht was under construction on one of the slipways. Inland, as winter gave way to spring, and spring to a glorious summer, the ripening cornfields threw a sheet of gold across the countryside.

Gordon's responsibilities were concerned with drawing plans for the forts. They were remote buildings strung out near the entrance to the harbour; seven miles from the nearest town and fifteen from the nearest station. As he told his parents, he pitied the men who'd have to live in them. Socially, his surroundings seem to have had little to commend them. Pembroke was, he announced in a letter home, 'the most gossiping place in Europe'. Not that it mattered much to him. He bought a horse and gig and spent much of his leisure, which began at 2 p.m. each afternoon, in touring the countryside with a captain of the 11th Regiment named Drew. He also became friendly with the local ferryman who, years afterwards, still remembered how he used to cross the stream by walking through the water.

Captain Drew deserves more than he has received from posterity. He is like a figure in a photograph, that has been under-exposed and has not quite come out. We know that he was married, and that his wife was one of the few women whom Gordon liked – for whom he even felt a small affection. We also know that he was an intensely religious man, and that most of their talk on the outings in the gig was devoted to spiritual matters. Apart from this, the faceless captain seems to have been cast in the role of a catalyst between Gordon and the Almighty – no doubt assisted by that never tiring correspondent, Augusta, who was prepared to advance the cause of her faith at the slightest encouragement.

The wild young man who was Charles Gordon was left behind at the military academy. At Pembroke, another Gordon appeared and anyone who studied him carefully could, perhaps, see the makings of the saint. Although he had never been confirmed, and never was, he began to attend Holy Communion. He thanked providence that he was 'free from the temptations of a line regiment, [because] I am such a miserable wretch, that I should be sure to be led away.' He recalled to Augusta how he used to laugh when the postman brought her supplies of devotional literature; but 'thank God it is different with me now. I feel much happier and more contented than I used to do.' In one letter of enthusiasm at his newfound faith, he told her: 'No novels or worldly books come up to the Sermons of McCheyne or the Commentaries of Scott' – a statement which many would have disputed, but which is an indication of the changes which Pembrokeshire, Captain and Mrs Drew, and sister Augusta had wrought in the young officer's character. It was, perhaps, fortunate that Gordon the soldier still existed. Otherwise, this phase might have been the makings of Gordon the insufferable prig.

Meanwhile, his father had been posted to Gibraltar. When not delving into religious literature, Gordon was an avid newspaper reader; and, when he had done with them, he used to send them on to the family. One paper of which he particularly approved, and which he often referred to in his letters, was a sheet named *Jackson's Journal*. He also concerned himself with his parents' spiritual welfare. 'Dear Father and Mother,' he wrote, 'think of eternal things.' All of which no doubt pleased mother, but may have surprised father.

If Gordon's life at this time was bounded by the construction of forts on one side, and by religion on the other, the country as a whole had more pressing concerns. In March of that year, the Crimean War broke out. Not since Wellington had beaten Bonaparte at Waterloo had the nation been involved in a major conflict. For thirty-nine years, the British army had stagnated, growing sluggish from disuse, and more concerned with the peacockry of the parade ground, than with the realities of modern warfare. Even at the moment when thousands of troops were landing on the Crimean peninsula, and beginning what was to be, for many, the last march of their lives, the War Office seemed to have little better to do than to send out directives about a new full dress uniform for officers. One of them reached Gordon at his South Wales outpost. It was, he observed,

> a great nuisance, as my coat is almost new, and I am afraid it will not alter into a tunic. We are to keep our frock-coat which is to be open in front, with a red waistcoat; our gold lace trousers are to be dispensed with, but the cocked hat is to be retained.

Throughout his career, he had a great dislike of any favouritism he might receive as a result of his family's connections with the army. When, on 30 November, he opened orders telling him to depart for Corfu, he concluded that his mother had been guilty of this offence. 'I suspect,' he wrote to her, 'you used your interest to have me sent there instead of to the Crimea. It is a great shame of you. However, I must not grumble, as I am lucky in not being sent to the West Indies, or New Zealand.'

One of the tenets of his new faith was a kind of fatalism: an overriding belief that everything was ordered by God and that everything, even if it might not seem to be, was for the best. As a token of his newly realized dependence on the Supreme Plan, he developed the habit of inserting the initials 'DV' in his letters whenever he talked about the future. He would do this, or that would happen to him, he explained – but only if God wished it. Nevertheless, he was ready enough to assist the Almighty in any attempt he might make to modify this plan. What is more, if Mrs Gordon was prepared to fight unfairly by bringing influence to work on his career, he was not too proud to adopt the same tactics. In a letter addressed to Sir John Burgoyne, the inspector-general of fortifications and an old friend of the family, he pleaded eloquently to be allowed to go on active service. His argument must have appealed to the old general. The posting to Corfu was cancelled. On 4 December he received fresh instructions – this time ordering him to Balaclava. Two days later, he had bought himself a supply of warm clothing, and was down at Portsmouth. The saint, who had been so busy assembling materials for his homemade religion, would have to retire for the time being. Lieutenant C. G. Gordon, RE, had work to do. The soldier was doing what soldiers should do: going to a war.

2
The Baptism of Fire

Gordon's orders were to transport three hundred and twenty huts to Balaclava and, once he was there, to erect them. He described them as 'rather pretty in appearance'. Each would accommodate twenty-two men, or four subalterns and two captains, or two field officers, or one general. The only pity was that they had not been dispatched earlier. As the *Illustrated London News* tartly commented in its first issue of 1855:

> An army of heroes ... was left to perish from cold, hunger and disease; not by an ungrateful or careless country, but in consequence of the defective administration of the army by the authorities at home – by the want of organization – by the incompatability of existing means to the desired ends – and by the obstinate adherence of men in office to rusty formalities and effete routine.

The Times was no less scathing. 'The Year,' its leader writer observed, 'has overturned our faith in many things, shaken many convictions, and dissipated many illusions.'

But the young sapper subaltern, who was busy loading sections of the huts on board ship at Portsmouth, was in no mood to criticize. When he had received the directive about new uniforms, he was not concerned about its irrelevance – but, rather, whether he could afford to make the changes. His present preoccupations were a mixture of excitement at the impending adventure, and concern at the problems of getting there. His instructions were that he should travel with the huts on board a collier which had been chartered to transport them. This prospect was a great deal more ominous than the thought of possible perils at the end of the voyage. He had no fear of enemy bullets: indeed, he said in later life that he had gone to the Crimea in the hope of being killed. With his new-found religious faith, an early death meant less time on earth, and a longer eternity in heaven. Much as he might welcome his own demise, however, he was less prepared for the rigours of a long sea voyage. Whenever it came on to blow, Charles Gordon was abominably seasick.

Even though he disliked any hint of favouritism, he was now goaded by desperation. He asked the War Office for permission to travel independently of the huts: to take a train to Marseilles and then to travel on a somewhat larger French ship. The authorities agreed, but even this apparently happy solution to his worries had a snag. He had, it seemed, to pay for his passage, and this offended the thrifty instincts which had been so carefully drilled into him by his father. 'If I had known this,' he told his parents, 'I should have thought twice about it.' After all, the fare from Marseilles to Constantinople was £17, and he was determined to exist on his pay without any help from his family. But it was now too late for second thoughts. At 8.30 p.m. on 14 December, he boarded a train from London to Paris.

The voyage from Marseilles to the Turkish capital took six and a half days. He had no complaints about it, though he was unhappy about the three hundred and twenty French soldiers who were on board without any shelter. If British troops had been exposed to such conditions, he noted, they would have mutinied. The Frenchmen, on the other hand, seemed to accept the situation with cheerful resignation.

Gordon's skill as a mapmaker, his talent as a surveyor and, as became clear later, the thoroughness and imagination with which he carried out reconnaissance, made him a natural tourist. If he had not gone into the army, he would surely have found a position in Herr Baedekker's flourishing guide book industry. Wherever he went, he insisted on seeing, as it were, behind the scenes. He studied the place and its people with extreme interest – he made innumerable drawings, and asked many questions. He was, in a word, inquisitive.

The trip to Constantinople made a change from the Pembrokeshire landscape. When the ship called at Messina on 22 December, he was told that the city had recently succumbed to that scourge of the nineteenth century, cholera. Twenty-two thousand of its sixty-six thousand population had died, but this did not prevent him from going ashore and studying the aftermath of the epidemic. No doubt he was anxious to find out as much as he could about it, for the disease was rampant in the Crimea. Whenever a Russian sniper missed his target, he could comfort himself with the thought that the bug would probably get his intended victim in the end.

At Constantinople ('I must say I was rather disappointed with the view'), he had to wait until the steamer carrying the huts had passed through the straits. The Duke of Cambridge was staying in one of the hotels, and Gordon sent him his regards. But if he had hoped that this high-ranking officer would invite him round for a chat about the gay old days on Corfu, he was to be disappointed. The duke had other things on his mind.

Eventually, the collier passed by on her way to the Black Sea, and Gordon embarked in a vessel named the *Golden Fleece* for the trip to Balaclava. He arrived at the Russian port on New Year's Day, 1855.

The chief sources of information about Gordon's experiences in the Crimea are his letters home. As a record of fact, they are no doubt impeccable: as a record of his opinions, on the other hand, some of the passages may be suspect. They were written with Mrs Gordon in mind, and he was constantly at pains to reassure his mother that he was well fed, in excellent health, and in no danger. The reassurances were not confined to himself. His brother Enderby was out there, serving with a battery of gunners, and brother Henry was working with the commissariat. The three of them met from time to time, and after these encounters, a letter usually left Balaclava for England where his father was now stationed.

One of his letters made haste to report 'no volunteering for me, as I have nothing to gain'. In another, he tells his mother that 'as far as comfort is concerned, I assure you, my dear – I could not be more comfortable in England.' He does once permit himself to observe that he found something 'indescribably exciting in war', but he urges her not to pay too much attention to reports in the press. They were, he wrote, 'atrocious fibs'. He noted that *The Times* correspondent, William Howard Russell, was occupying a comfortable house at Balaclava; but he did not mention that the commander-in-chief, Lord Raglan, was similarly installed, and that the general was protecting himself against the rigours of the Crimean winter by staying indoors. When, later in the year, his lordship died of cholera, he received the customary panaegyrics which the Victorians lavished on the dear departed. Many people, including Gordon, remarked on what a kind man he had been, and there was a sudden concern for the future of the campaign – now that he was gone. At the beginning of the year, however, one correspondent was noting his absence from the field of combat, and was telling his readers that 'Lord Raglan lives in his house for days together and is not visible'. It was, he suggested, hardly a state of affairs which would inspire confidence in the badly misused troops.

Gordon himself had a talent for living rough, and asked for very little in the way of creature comforts. He condemned the roads as 'bad beyond description', but this was mainly because they made it difficult to get his huts up to the front. By contrast, he was almost casual in his reference to two officers of another regiment who had been frozen to death – and to three members of a foot regiment, who had been 'smothered with charcoal fumes so I shall keep a sharp look out not to use it'.

For the moment, he, too, was comfortably billeted in a house, and surrounded by 'a great many friends'. When he went about his duties, however, he must have witnessed the appalling scenes which were reported in the British press, and which, in spite of what he said, were by no means the products of imaginative journalists. Less than a month earlier, another officer had written to a friend in England that 'our misery, my dear fellow, exceeds anything you have yet read of it.' And, from an NCO: 'The first view of Balaclava is not very encouraging to a young beginner. Dead horses, broken carts, waggons, etc., are all strewn about the quay. The soldiers are in tatters: blankets have been converted into leggings, and there are no shoes.'

The snow was over a foot deep, and the one blessing of the cold was that it put a firm crust of ice on the roads. At the merest hint of a thaw, they became quagmires of mud. Officers, on Gordon's admission, were to be seen foraging for food, and none of them revealed the smallest concern for the welfare of their men. According to *The Times*: 'The officer does not give himself the slightest trouble in the world about the fate of the private, his food, dress, or shelter; he leaves all that to the commissariat.' And the commissariat was not able to cope. A previous consignment of huts was lying in the mud on Balaclava quay – simply because those responsible for their despatch from England had forgotten to include any nails. Florence Nightingale once claimed that she was 'now clothing the British Army', which was only just short of the truth. When Gordon condemned the press, he was doubtless echoing the view of many, more senior, officers, who were jealous of the honour of their service – and outraged by the inefficiency which had spoilt its reputation. When William Howard Russell arrived on the scene, one general remarked: 'By God, Sir, I'd as soon see the devil.' They did not, it seemed, mind how bad things were – provided nobody in England knew about it. It was better to be destitute than dishonoured.

From the docks at Balaclava, the distance to the front line was only eight miles. When Gordon arrived, an engineer promised him that a railway, which was under construction, would be ready in six weeks. As things turned out, it took longer; though, by the summer, two small locomotives (one of them named the *Victory*) were chuffing busily up and down the line. This did not, however, assist the task of transporting the huts to the place where they were so badly needed. During the first few days, only two were erected, and Gordon fretted at the delay. Nevertheless, he comforted himself with the thought that the two pairs of chamois leather vests and drawers he had brought with him were doing an excellent job of keeping out the cold. He met the dreaded Russell of *The Times*; took the opportunity to visit his brothers; and as always, took a keen interest in his surroundings. Balaclava was quiet. 'We hear a gun now and then,' he wrote in one of his letters, 'but they are generally fired by the Russians at the French.' There were, he thought 'no hardships for the officers; the men are the sufferers, and that is partly their own fault ... they are like children, thinking everything is to be done for them.' Presently, a body of fifteen hundred Croats arrived to manhandle the sections of the huts up to the forward areas and he was able to begin work in earnest. He had already noticed that the 'country near Sebastopol is so like the Downs, and the climate also is so similar, that we can scarcely believe we are in Russia.' On 18 January, he had his first view of the beleagured city itself.

I do not think I ever saw a prettier city [he wrote]. It looks quite open, and a Russian steamer was cruising about inside the harbour. Two of their steamers came out the other day and bombarded the French lines for two hours, but our vessels were unable to move out to attack them, as their steam was not up.

After three weeks, the last of the huts had been erected, and Gordon was ordered to the trenches. He was still, he made haste to reassure his mother, comfortable. He had a double tent, sunk two feet into the ground, with the earth heaped up outside it. He was also wise to the old campaigner's trick of getting hold of an empty beer barrel and cutting it in two. One half was turned upside down, and with a coat draped over it, served as a chair. The other offered a passable substitute for a bath. The main problem was the cost of bread, which was priced at 2s. 0d. for a small loaf.

The French, who were quartered nearby, were much better organized. As Gordon said, 'the French soldier looks after himself and consequently fares much better'. Indeed, there was a saying that 'the Englishmen always asked for brandy and champagne, while the Frenchmen asked for needles and thread'. Their tents were laid out in neat rows, and they had made some effort to beat the mud by paving the roads. They had their own bakeries, which gave them a plentiful supply of bread (the British troops had to rely on biscuits, which were reputed to cause scurvy), and their morale was high. The Zouaves were especially adventurous. They used to creep over to the enemy lines at night, and drape French flags over the Russian outworks. If you asked them when Sebastopol would be taken, however, they were pessimistic. 'When there are three Thursdays in a week!' was a popular Zouave estimate.

Gordon's first taste of action occurred on 14 February, when he was on duty in the trenches. The French were intending to establish a forward position in a ruined house. The building was, however, vulnerable on one of its flanks. Using a small ravine, the Russians could approach it under cover and take it with little difficulty. The answer was to dig a line of weapon pits connecting the ruin with a nearby hill. In the side of the latter, there were some caves. Gordon was detailed to take a working-party of eight men, and to see that the pits were dug.

If he had told the men to get on with the job, while he waited in the cover of the trenches, it would have occasioned no criticism. Many other officers carried out their duties in just such a manner, but this was not to be Gordon's way. If there was any action to be had, he wanted to be in it. He certainly never believed that a commander should lead his men from behind. Not without difficulty, he managed to get hold of the eight men and the necessary picks and shovels. He led them up to a forward trench, where he found a captain on duty. The officer made no secret of the fact that he had only recently arrived in the Crimea; that he knew little about active service, and that he was not very anxious to fill this gap in his experience. By contrast, Gordon kept quiet about his own background – preferring to imply by saying little that he was a battle-hardened veteran.

He told the captain the situation, and asked him to post sentries in no-man's-land. He pointed out the caves in particular, which he thought might be occupied by the Russians. If there was any danger in the mission, this was where it would come from. The officer grunted his consent: called over an NCO, and told him to get on with the job.

Gordon set off at nightfall, cautiously leading his eight men over rough ground which was now coated with a film of ice. His first concern was to make sure that the sentries had secured the caves. When he reached them, he discovered that they had not. There were no soldiers there – and, consequently, no guarantee that the Russians were not lurking inside, waiting for an opportunity to spring a trap. Telling the troops to wait, he wandered off to inspect them. There was a smell of stale air, a chilly feeling of damp, but no Russians. So far, so good: he found the sentries, who were quietly killing time under cover, and hoping that nothing would happen. He directed two of them to the high ground above the caves: saw them into position, and then returned to post another pair at the bottom of the hill. He was explaining their duties, when a couple of shots hit the ground nearby. They had been fired by the two men on the higher ground, who had mistaken them for the enemy. Having made this brief gesture, they promptly bolted back to the cover of the trenches. The working party showed every sign of being about to follow their example, but Gordon restrained them. He was less successful with the other sentries, who refused to move forward.

The two shots had alerted a Russian position about a hundred and fifty yards away. As Gordon and his frightened men went out to begin the real business of the night, they were greeted by a shower of bullets. Fortunately nobody was hit and, having established their presence, the Russians made no further attempt to harass the working party. No doubt taking

32

comfort that here, at last, was an officer who was prepared to share the hazards of campaigning, the men carried out their task with efficiency. During the night, Gordon went down into the ravine, where he found that the French, too, were busy.

Having told them who we were, [Gordon wrote after-wards] I returned to the trench, where I met Colonel ————— of the 1st Royals. I warned him if he went out he would be sure to be hit by our own sentries or the Russians. He would go, however, and a moment afterwards was hit in the breast, the ball going through his coats, slightly grazing his ribs, and passing out again without hurting him. I stayed with my working-party all night, and got home very tired.

On another occasion, he found some soldiers cowering in a trench without so much as an NCO in charge of them. The men were completely demoralized, and the enemy could have walked over them without their noticing it. Gordon, who was only armed with a swagger stick, decided to keep them company. Throughout the next hour or so he deliberately exposed himself over the earthworks: seeming to invite the enemy to fire at him. The unhappy infantrymen were encouraged by his example. After watching it for a while, they began to take a more intelligent interest in the war.

Gordon went through the Crimean War with the bravado which comes from a feeling of being invulnerable – and, at the same time, not very much minding what might happen to him. On one occasion, a Russian shell landed five yards away, but it failed to go off. On another, a near miss only produced the comment that the enemy were 'very good marksmen; their bullet is large and pointed'. In the official accounts of the war, he is reported as having been wounded, though this is something of an exaggeration. An enemy round chipped off a fragment of stone, which hit him on the head and stunned him for a second or two. By the time he received treatment, he had recovered sufficiently to make a joke of trying to light a cigar from the red hair of the surgeon. It may not have been very funny, but it seems to have raised a laugh. Later he told his parents that 'old Jones [the Chief Royal Engineer] had persisted in returning me as wounded'.

Of more interest to him was an armistice which was arranged with the Russians on 31 March to enable both sides to bury their dead. This gave him an opportunity to study the enemy at close quarters. 'The Russian officers came over and talked to us,' he reported. He noticed that 'they did not look particularly clean', but he thought none the less of their ability for this. They 'certainly are inferior to none', he wrote.

Winter turned to spring: new grass pushed its way through what remained of the old, and crocuses made their appearance. Then it was summer, and the commander-in-chief determined to attack Sebastopol. The key to the conquest was the capture of two forts on high ground at the south-western edge of the city: the Redan and the Malakoff. If these fell, the rest would fall: the allied forces would be able to march into the docks and destroy the magnificent naval base. Russia would be crippled as a sea power in the Mediterranean, and the war would, to all intents and purposes, be over.

During the first week in June, the French made an assault on the Malakoff, and nearly reached the tower which was the fort's main feature. They were driven off by heavy gunfire, while the British stood by and watched. This, Gordon believed, was a mistake. 'If we had liked to assault,' he wrote home, 'I am sure we should have taken the place with little loss, some of our men being so close to the Redan.' Ten days later, the allies tried again.

The engineers reported for their briefing in General Jones's hut on 16 June. The French, once again, were to attack the Malakoff: the British were to pit their strength against the Redan. They were to advance in three columns, each of which was to be led by an officer of the Royal Engineers and ten sappers equipped with tools for removing obstacles. A covering party of one hundred infantrymen would march behind them; then troops carrying bags of wool to place over barbed

34

wire; then a ladder party; and, finally, the main column. The attack was scheduled to begin at daybreak (3 a.m.) on the 17th, when an artillery barrage would open up. It would be sustained for three hours until, at 6 a.m., the troops would go in. Gordon, with Lieutenants Murray and Graham, was to travel with the first column under the command of a Major Brent.

Late on the evening of the 17th, however, the plan was suddenly modified. The French general was impatient at the losses his men were sustaining in the trenches. He had no intention of waiting what seemed to be an unnecessary three hours for the artillery to soften the defences. He proposed to go in at dawn, and the British would oblige him by doing likewise.

Even then, the French mistook a random outbreak of firing for shots of an eight-gun battery, which had been detailed to give the signal to begin operations. They went over the starting line ten minutes too soon, and all attempts to synchronize movements were thrown into chaos. By the time the British went into the attack, the Russians were prepared for them. In the carnage which followed, neither the British nor the French achieved anything worth talking about, and certainly nothing worth the price of the terrible casualty list.

Gordon had been on duty in the trenches all day on the 16th. At seven in the evening, he went back for dinner – where he was told to be ready for duty again at midnight. He was instructed to report in one of the advanced trenches, about two hundred yards from the Redan. Once the signal had been given for the British attack, the Russians opened up a murderous fire of grapeshot. The men huddled together in the trenches were (Gordon's words) 'mown down in dozens'. Had the troops broken out of the trenches and gone into the attack, he believed that the outcome would have been very different. They might have taken the Redan: there would undoubtedly have been fewer casualties. 'Every yard nearer would have diminished the effect of the grape by giving it less space for spreading,' he wrote. 'We could then have moved up our supports and carried the place.'

But the men did not break out: they dribbled out. About one hundred of them reached the foot of the fort. Unfortunately, there was nobody to back them up, and they had to retire. Meanwhile, the French were driven back from the Malakoff, and Raglan decided not to renew the assault. With the Malakoff still in Russian hands, it would have been impossible to take the Redan.

In Gordon's column, Murray went out with the skirmishers. He could be seen distinctly, a red-coated figure running beside the green-clad riflemen. He did not survive for long. Gordon wrote:

> He was not out a minute when he was carried back with his arm shattered with grape. Colonel Tylden called for me, and asked me to look after him, which I did, and as I had a tourniquet in my pocket I put it on. He bore it bravely, and I got a stretcher and had him taken back. He died three hours afterwards. I am glad to say that Dr Brent reports that he did not die from loss of blood, but from the shock, not being very strong.

The withdrawal began at 7 a.m., but it was noon before the sappers received their instructions to move back.

The routine of siege warfare was resumed. Gordon was busy with his engineering duties: building new batteries and repairing old ones; constructing platforms for mortars; supervising the digging of saps in readiness for the next assault; making countless drawings, and writing long letters home. He was seldom out of danger. At night, there was the constant likelihood of Russian raids. As *The Times* man wrote, 'A man stands in great danger every time he enters the works; but it would never do to be continually thinking of this.' There were two hundred men on one of Gordon's working parties. By the end of the night, thirty had been killed or wounded. The hours of duty were long – especially when, at one time, all the other officers in his unit were ill. For over a month, he was compelled to work twenty hours a day. 'It gets tedious after a time,' he wrote home, 'but if anything is going on, one does not mind.'

Throughout this period, he built up a remarkable store of knowledge about the geography of both the Allied and Russian lines. Some while afterwards, a lieutenant-colonel from an infantry regiment wrote:

> I happened to mention to Charlie Gordon that I was field officer for the day for command in the trenches next day, and, having only just returned from sick leave, that I was ignorant of the geography of our left attack. He said at once, 'Oh! come down with me tonight after dark, and I will show you over the trenches.' He drew me out a very clear sketch of the lines . . . and down I went accordingly. He explained every nook and corner, and took me outside our most advanced trench, the bouquets* and other missiles flying about us in, to me, a very unpleasant manner, but he taking the mattter remarkably coolly.

Throughout this period, he gave few indications of the religious conversion which had been such a feature of his life at Pembroke. He took Holy Communion, but so did many other officers. He showed a magnificent disregard for the hazards of warfare, but he was certainly not the only courageous young officer in the Crimea. During his time off duty, he enjoyed riding over to Inkermann, and he once observed that he would like to be back in England for the partridge shooting. He was undoubtedly very efficient at his work: when the campaign was over, the Chief Royal Engineer commended him with ten other subalterns for having 'particularly distinguished themselves'. The French presented him with the Legion of Honour, but this award should not be taken too seriously. Many other officers received it: it was more a reward for being an ally, than a recognition of any particular act of gallantry.

On 8 September, the French made another assault on the Malakoff; and, this time succeeded. The tricolour was hoisted

* Clusters of small shells fired from mortars.

to the top of the tower. After an operation which cost them a prodigious number of men (including four generals), the key to Sebastopol was theirs. A British assault on the Redan failed – largely, in Gordon's opinion, because of the commanders' failure to press home their advantages. They were retiring when they should have been going forward. The Highlanders were ordered to renew the offensive on the following morning, when Gordon was detailed for trench duty.

But the Russians had had enough.

During the night [Gordon wrote] I heard terrible explosions, and going down to the trenches at 4 p.m. I saw a splendid sight – the whole town in flames, and every now and then a terrific explosion. The rising sun shone on the scene of destruction producing a beautiful effect. The last of the Russians were leaving the town over the bridge.

Once Malakoff had fallen, it afterwards transpired, the Russians became concerned about their lines of communication. They had begun to evacuate the city at midnight – leaving most of their guns behind.

Sightseeing in Sebastopol was discouraged for fear that the Russians had left booby-traps behind, and the city was declared out of bounds for forty-eight hours. Fortunately for the inveterate tourist in Gordon, he was free from such restrictions, for he had been assigned to make a plan of the Russian defences. He began by exploring the Redan – which, for so long, had been so desirable and unattainable.

He managed to remove a Russian gunsight as a souvenir for his father, also some cups and other trivia for his mother and sisters. Otherwise, he reported, there was 'an extraordinary rarity of knick-knacks. They left their pictures in the churches, which form consequently the only spoil, and which I do not care about buying.' Otherwise 'there was nothing but rubbish and fleas'.

With the greater part of the Russian port in allied hands, the British and French engineers were faced with a considerable task. That great dockyard, which was the pride of the

Russian fleet and vital to the nation's role as a sea power, had to be destroyed. The magnificent theatre, the churches, and the avenues of mansions which, miraculously, it seemed, had survived the siege, might remain. The harbour had to be blasted to smithereens.

There were five docks in all; a basin twenty-seven feet above the sea, which the vessels entered by a short canal and three locks; and sundry fortifications. The French engineers were entrusted with the demolition of the two northern docks: the British were responsible for blowing up the three to the south. It took a long time and well over 100,000 pounds of high explosive to complete the task. In the course of this work, Gordon met several of his opposite numbers in the French army. They were, he noted, older than the British sappers, and their NCOs seemed to be more intelligent.

During this period, he left Sebastopol briefly to serve with the expedition which was sent to reduce Kinburn, one of the two Russian forts at the mouth of the Dneiper. If it had not been for the rough passage by sea, the outing might have been more of a rest cure, for Kinburn fell with a minimal show of opposition and his engineering skill was not required.

Back in Sebastopol, autumn dragged into winter. On 15 December, there was a heavy rainstorm. On the following day, the first severe frosts came. Gordon went about his business of blowing things up – and thinking about the future. He was not anxious to go back to Britain, since there was 'no allurement in the home duties of our people'. On the other hand, if he remained abroad, he would have preferred it to be in a war zone. The excitement, the uncertainty, and the need for self-sufficiency had appealed to him no end. And, which must have satisfied the thrifty instincts of Gordons father and son, he had managed to live through the campaign and its aftermath with only the smallest help from his family. The sum of his requests from home had amounted to a new forage cap, a map of the Crimea and a bottle of Rowland's Odonto (some sort of patent medicine, presumably). When dispatching this small order, Mrs Gordon had added a bottle of cherry brandy.

Gordon need not have worried about a home posting. The War Office had no intention of sending him back to Britain. His ability as a surveyor had not gone unremarked; and, when the Crimean War formally came to an end with the Treaty of Paris in 1856, Europe had a new frontier to mark out. The genesis of the war had taken place, when Russia occupied Moldavia and Wallachia – provinces which had been ruled by the Ottoman Empire for three hundred years and which, with the coming of Russian troops, had extended the Tsar's domain as far as the mouth of the Danube.* It was now determined that Russia should be kept away from that river. The British member of the Commission charged with surveying the new frontier was a Colonel Stanton. Gordon was appointed to his staff in May 1856. For the first part of the assignment, he was stationed in Bessarabia. He had estimated that the work would last for six months. In fact, it took a year. When it was over, he was detailed for a similar task in Armenia. Using the new electric telegraph, which linked Constantinople to London, he appealed against the posting, but the War Office was adamant. 'Lieutenant Gordon must go,' the authorities cabled back.

Gordon found no particular enjoyment in civilized society, and this work made sure that he was kept away from it. He lived rough, carrying out his duties patiently – while the powers bickered over the precise frontier line, and local tribesmen showed a tiresome inclination to steal his instruments. The Turkish and Russian members of the commission were constantly fighting: the Russian wine was horrible, and he found the manners of his former enemies no better. As for the Turks, whenever their commissioner needed transport, he simply stopped a caravan, and commandeered the wretched travellers' horses. The Khurdish tribesmen excited his admira-

* Two years later, in 1858, Moldavia and Wallachia were amalgamated and a new principality named Roumania came into being.

tion for their magnificent disregard of authority. 'They are,' he wrote, 'as lawless as ever. They go from Turkey to Russia and back as they like; they are fine looking people, armed to the teeth.' He was less receptive to another tribe, which offered him prices ranging from £40 to £120 for anybody he might care to kidnap. The idea was to transport the victims to the slave market in Constantinople. During the previous eighteen months, sixty-two people had vanished into slavery. It was not a trade he felt inclined to encourage.

However, there were many compensations. The weather in winter was 'beautifully clear . . . capital for sledging'. There were expeditions to shoot wolves, which he enjoyed; and he came within a few thousand feet of climbing Mount Arrarat. On the other hand, there were over one hundred plans to be drawn ('I have had enough of them for my whole life'), and countless disputes about a harsh, rock-strewn territory of which he, Gordon, wouldn't 'take thirty square miles for a gift'. All in all, it was not without relief that the job came to an end, and he returned to Britain. He was home in time for Christmas 1858. He had, however, no intention of remaining there. 'I do not feel at all inclined to settle in England and be employed in any sedentary way,' he wrote. Even before he left Armenia, he had applied for a job at Baghdad, but it fell through. On 1 April 1859, he was promoted to captain. One month later he was given the post of adjutant to the Royal Engineers' depot at Chatham. If his ambitions had been more orthodox, he should have been glad. The appointment singled him out as an officer with a successful future ahead of him. But no— this was not the way of the world as Charles Gordon saw it. He would keep his eyes open for any opening which promised action – no matter how far away, nor how tenuously linked with the civilized world, it might be.

3

The Chinese Puzzle

Gordon passed the time at Chatham conscientiously if with no very great enthusiasm. He was continually looking for an opportunity which would take him abroad and into action. By the middle of 1860, a possibility presented itself. For many years, the relations between Britain and China had been in an almost continual state of war and near-war. For commercial reasons, the former was determined to import opium into China, whilst the Chinese Imperial authorities were equally intent on prohibiting it. The Emperor's objections were not unreasonable: the drug was undermining the health of his people and, especially, his army. It was, on the other hand, an important product of India, and a great deal of cash was at stake. The British government found it convenient to take the view that the Emperor's embargo was not made on any moral grounds. He was, the ministers told themselves, worried about the competition which imported supplies created for the homegrown product.

The Opium Wars were fought and, predictably, won by the British. According to the peace treaty, which was signed in 1858, opium smoking (and, therefore, its trade) was to be legalized throughout China. The Emperor was also called upon to overcome his dislike of foreigners, and to permit the presence of overseas diplomats in Peking. It was not a demand which he accepted with any relish – nor, as events were to show, had he any intention of observing it. After a great deal of argument, a British delegation set out for the Chinese capital at the beginning of 1860. As their ship entered the Peiho River, they were fired upon by Chinese troops occupying positions known as the Taku Forts. This rebuff was not to be tolerated. As Lord Palmerston told Parliament, we must 'bring John Chinaman to his bearings'. He was not alone in his determination. The French government, which had appointed itself protector of the Roman Catholic church beyond the seas, was exasperated by the recent murder of a missionary in Shanghai. It, too, would be delighted to join in the business of reorientating John Chinaman. The two nations agreed to send a joint expedition to Peking. Palmerston's only concern seems to have been that this might give the French troops a chance to study the new Enfield rifle which was being issued to the British army. But then he decided not to worry; the troops could take the old version with them. It would be good enough to bring the Chinese to their senses.

When Gordon read about the situation, he promptly wrote to the War Office, volunteering for active service. His application was accepted: on 22 July 1860, he sailed for the Far East. The ship reached Hong Kong in early September; and, on the 17th, he arrived in Shanghai. The small war was almost over: the one and only battle had been fought and, by the time he had moved up to Peking, the Anglo-French force was occupying a large expanse of ground in front of the city. During their retreat, the Chinese had taken a number of prisoners including diplomatic staff with them. The Emperor and his advisors were now resorting to the weapon they used with such dexterity when everything else had failed: argument. The immediate point at issue was their unwillingness to surrender the main gate. They had been given two days to make up their minds. Either they gave in unconditionally, or else the allies would batter their way in.

Gordon and the other sappers were ordered to throw up earthworks preparatory to an attack. While they were doing this, unpleasant rumours reached the Anglo-French lines. It seemed that the captured men had been treated well enough until they reached the Emperor's Summer Palace. Then with the ruler himself in attendance, they were said to have been handled with considerable brutality. 'Poor de Norman,' Gordon wrote, 'who was with me in Asia, is one of the victims. It appears that they were tied so tight by their wrists that the flesh mortified, and they died in the greatest torture.'

At 11.30 a.m. on 13 October, half an hour before the ultimatum expired, the giant gate at the entrance to the city was drawn open, but this was not the end of the negotiations. Having – symbolically, at any rate – surrendered Peking, the Chinese had now to consider the terms for a peace treaty. They were given a further ten days to think them over. In the meanwhile the reports about the prisoners were confirmed. A few had been released; but some had, indeed, been horribly put to death in the palace dungeons. Some sort of reprisal had to be devised, which would punish the Emperor without harming the rest of the Chinese people. The answer came from the British ambassador designate, Lord Elgin. What better idea, said His Lordship, than to destroy the most beautiful of all the Emperor's possessions: the very Summer Palace in which the atrocities had taken place. The French were shocked by such an act of overt vandalism just as, a few days later, the British were appalled by the looting of the palace by the French. On the other hand, Westminster – which meant Palmerston – heartily approved of the suggestion.

Gordon, who had little aesthetic sense, was nevertheless tremendously impressed by the building.

We accordingly went in [he wrote] and, after pillaging it, burned the whole place, destroying in a Vandal-like manner most valuable property which would not be replaced for four millions.

But the French were not to go uncriticized by him.

You could scarcely conceive the magnificence of this residence, or the tremendous devastation the French have committed. The throne room was lined in ebony, carved in a marvellous way. There were huge mirrors of all shapes and kinds, clocks, watches, musical boxes with puppets on them,

44

magnificent china of every description, heaps and heaps of silks of all colours, embroidery, and as much splendour and civilization as you would see at Windsor.

He was never a man to encourage plundering, but he records with almost a sense of wonder how one of his fellow officers bought a string of pearls for 16s. 0d., and sold it on the following day for £500. He himself purchased the Emperor's throne, which he shipped to England and presented to the headquarters of the Royal Engineers at Chatham.

Although there was plenty in Peking to occupy Gordon's zest for sightseeing, he was not happy in the city. The sacking of the palace was, he said, 'wretchedly demoralizing work for an army. Everyone was wild for plunder.' It was an act of revenge against the Emperor, and no doubt a very effective one. At all events, he died soon afterwards. His death, however, was not very much compensation to the relatives of those who had been murdered. For them, there were to be cash payments. According to the terms of the peace treaty, the Chinese were required to pay £10,000 for every Englishman who had died in captivity. Their native clerks and servants were less expensive: £500 apiece was deemed to be sufficient payment for their lives.

Gordon found the inhabitants of the city civil enough on the surface, though naturally there was a detectable undercurrent of hatred, when the palace, its two hundred summer houses, and a wealth of its works of art, all went up in smoke. Whilst Gordon had neither questioned nor criticized the orders, he was uncomfortably aware that there was a certain justification for this resentment. When the treaty was ratified, and the troops were withdrawn to Tientsin, he experienced a feeling of relief.

The majority of the soldiers soon went home, but there had to be some guarantee that the Manchu authorities would pay the reparations. Consequently, a force of three thousand was left behind at Tientsin under the command of General Sir Charles Staveley. Gordon's elder brother, Henry, was married to the general's sister. He, himself, was attached to Staveley's staff to supervise the building of barracks and stables. He was also put in charge of the administration of a fund which had been raised for the benefit of the Chinese poor.

What should have been a generous gesture ended in tragedy. When nine hundred dollars had been collected, the local mandarins were asked to issue tickets to the most deserving cases. This they refused to do, and when the day came to distribute the money, no fewer than three thousand beggars turned up. Alas – the system of crowd control broke down. In the rush to help themselves to this sudden and providential bounty, the paupers of Tientsin went wild. Seven women and one small boy were trampled to death in the crush.

For most of the time, the eighteen months Gordon spent at Tientsin were a pleasant interlude. Since he was responsible direct to Staveley, he was almost his own master, and he enjoyed this. The work was not very arduous, and he had plenty of opportunities for seeing the countryside. He explored the Great Wall of China with a fellow officer and a young Chinese boy, who acted as servant and interpreter. On several occasions, he rode the forty miles to the mouth of the Peiho river, where he inspected the Taku forts. He spent a week at the British legation in Peking, and he studied with interest the preparations which were made to immortalize the now dead Emperor.

A marble block, weighing 60 tons is being removed from the quarries to the west of Peking to the cemetery in the east. It is drawn along upon a huge truck by six hundred ponies, and proceeds at the rate of four miles a day. When it arrives, it is to be set up and carved into the shape of an elephant; several other large stones are also *en route.*

His health was usually exceptionally good, but he succumbed to a mild attack of smallpox. Medically, it was without significance; spiritually, the days on his sick bed, and the attentions of the garrison chaplain, who was 'excessively kind', brought back echoes of those days at Pembroke. One has to suppose that the busy life he had led since touring the South Wales countryside with the devout Captain Drew had, if not exactly eroded his faith, then at least relegated it to the background. There had been too much to do, too much to see, to indulge in pious introspection. Now, he was able to report triumphantly in a letter to sister Augusta, 'this disease has brought me back to my Saviour, and I trust in future to be a better Christian than I have been hitherto.' In Gordon there was, perhaps, a saint struggling to get out, but the warrior was still keeping his other self in check. Nobody was more aware of this than he. He told Augusta, 'I am at present, two men: the one violent, brutal, hard, and in every way despicable; the other would hurt no one.' The resolution of this conflict would have to wait for a year or so; for, once again, events were about to overwhelm his religious inclinations. On 28 April 1862, he left Tientsin to join Staveley and the rest of the garrison, who had already moved to Shanghai. He arrived in the city on 3 May.

When he had passed through Shanghai on his way to the war which was not really a war at all, Gordon had noticed a macabre collection of human heads hanging in baskets from the city walls. These were the all too mortal remains of so-called Taiping rebels, who had been captured and, according to Chinese custom, decapitated. The exhibition was, presumably, to discourage others from joining their ranks. The rebellion was eleven years old at the time, and still flourishing. Indeed, the Anglo-French operation against Peking had given it a new lease of life, for it had weakened forces which the Emperor had deployed against it.

The instigator was a village schoolmaster named Huo-hsin, who was embittered by his failure to get into the Chinese civil service. During a serious illness, he dreamed that he had come face to face with God. Afterwards, he professed that the Almighty had told him that he was the younger brother of Jesus. Before very long, he began to call himself Tien Wang, or 'Heavenly King'. He was, he told his followers, about to introduce the Taiping ('Great Peace'), which was a euphemistic name for a bloodthirsty revolt aimed at toppling the Manchu dynasty. He appointed lieutenants to help him in the struggle, and he called them Wangs (Kings).

The foreign powers were not unduly perturbed about the Taiping Rebellion. They had the word of the missionaries that Tien Wang had been brought up as a Christian and that, therefore, he must be good. Furthermore they were not averse to anything which threatened the Emperor, who had shown himself to be a stubborn and slippery adversary. It was only when the Taipings began to menace the port of Shanghai, that anybody began to worry. Shanghai was the gateway to trade: the place where the money came from. So long as the bankers and merchants could count their gold in peace, they did not care much what went on in the rest of China. But when the Taipings seemed to be closing in on the city, they began to worry. There were terrible – and, as it happened, true – stories of what the rebels did to their prisoners. They either flayed them alive; or, if the mood took them, pounded them to death; or, a trick which their leader had doubtless picked up from his reading of the New Testament, crucified them. What was more, the presence of the Taipings in a neighbourhood was enough to guarantee that it would be pillaged, its crops destroyed, and a rich, food-producing, countryside would be reduced to something little better than a desert.

Nothing more than a token force of overseas troops was stationed in Shanghai, and so the European residents had to look to their own resources. Hitherto, many of them had obliged the rebels by supplying them with ammunition. The practice would have to cease; but this embargo, in itself, was far from sufficient. What they needed, they decided, was their own army. They gave an American soldier of fortune named Frederick T. Ward the task of recruiting and training it. To invest it with the image of success, they called it 'The Ever Victorious Army'. Ward appointed a fellow American, H. E. Burgevine, as his second-in-command. The European community raised funds for the cause and, encouraged by Li

Hung Chang, the governor of the province, so did the Chinese. Ward was, by all accounts, a good leader, and he did his best with what, despite its grandiose name, was little more than a rabble of troops, made up mostly of men belonging to no fixed nationality. The officers were a collection of ex-patriate Americans, Frenchmen and Germans. Most of them were heavy drinkers, and one estimate suggests that eleven out of the original hundred and forty died of DTs.

The Taipings continued to advance towards the city, until they were only ten miles away. At this point, it became clear that, if Shanghai were to continue its role as trading house of the Far East, rather more substantial measures would be needed. The British government was appealed to. Palmerston, who had praised the sacking of the Summer Palace, had to do a swift re-think. Now he was being asked to take measures which would help the Imperial power against its enemies. He decided that 'it cannot be for the advantages of those who trade with China that the country should be in a state of civil war.' There was, therefore, much to be said for suppressing the rebellion, and he agreed that General Staveley and his force should be sent to Shanghai, and that they should be instructed to clear the rebels away from an area within a radius of thirty miles from the city.

A well-drilled force of British regulars was a much more formidable opposition than the ill-disciplined ranks of The Ever Victorious Army, or the somewhat dispirited Imperialist troops. Gordon arrived in Shanghai a few days after Staveley and the main force; and, in even this brief period, one key town had already been recaptured from the rebels. He was just in time to take charge of a small detachment of sappers in readiness for the attack on Tsingpu – a city on the western perimeter of the zone.

The force began its thirty-mile march on the 6 May. It was raining heavily and, as they travelled farther and farther from the city, the depredations of the rebels became all too apparent. There was not a soul to be seen; the villages had been burnt to the ground; and the huge expanse of flat country, which should have been thick with ripening crops, was a wilderness. By the 10th, they had reached a point one and a half miles from the walls which enclosed Tsingpu. The column was halted and Staveley set about his reconnaissance. He took with him that past-master of sightseeing, Charles Gordon.

General Staveley takes over the narrative.

Captain Gordon was of the greatest use to me . . . He reconnoitred the enemy's defences and arranged for the ladder-parties to cross the moats, and for the escalating of the works; for we had to attack and carry by storm several towns fortified with high walls and deep wet ditches. He was, however, a source of much anxiety to me, from the daring manner he approached the enemy's works to acquire information. Previous to our attack upon Tsingpu, and when with me in a boat, reconnoitring the place, he begged to land, in order better to see the nature of the defences; presently, to my dismay, I saw him gradually going nearer and nearer, by rushes, from cover to cover, until he got behind a small outlying pagoda, within a hundred yards of the wall, and here he was quietly making a sketch and taking notes. I, in the meantime, was shouting myself hoarse in trying to get him back; for not only were the rebels firing at him from the walls, but I saw a party stealing round to cut him off.

On the night of the 11th, the guns were brought up into position. At daybreak, the artillerymen opened fire. Tons of brickwork came crashing down, and the town fell with no losses to Staveley's troops. The method was similar to that of many, similar, engagements: a quick march to the objective; a careful reconnaissance designed to discover the weakest point in the defences; a bombardment from as short a range as possible; and then the final assault.

Gordon noted that the Taipings were

a very funny people; they always run when attacked; they are ruthlessly cruel, and have a system of carrying off small boys under the hope of training them up as rebels. We always found swarms of these boys who had been taken from their parents (whom the rebels had killed) in the provinces.

Gordon was kind to these children, and took a number of them under his protection. Six of them, at various times, served as his orderlies, and at least one of them was educated at his expense. In an engagement under Staveley, he fished out a toddler who had fallen into a ditch while trying to escape. 'For which', he recorded, 'he rewarded me by destroying my coat with his muddy paws in clinging to me.'

By the end of the month, Staveley had driven the rebels out of five towns and his assignment was finished. The countryside had been purged of rebels, and the merchants in Shanghai could sleep more soundly at nights. He withdrew his force to the city, and ordered Gordon to prepare a thorough survey of the thirty-mile area. It was, he discovered, flat and fertile, with huge skies, and criss-crossed by a labyrinth of waterways. What was more to the point, however, was the fact that this work hardened his attitude to the Taipings. Whatever sympathy he may have had for their cause was quickly dispelled.

The people . . . are suffering greatly [he reported] and dying from starvation; this state of affairs is most sad, and the rebellion ought to be put down. Words cannot express the horrors these people suffer, or the utter desert they have made of this rich province. It is all very well to talk of non-intervention . . .

Although they had been cleared away from the area around Shanghai, the Taipings were still in control of nearly fourteen thousand square miles. While the Heavenly King languished in comfort at Nanking, a military base, under Chung Wang, was established a hundred miles away at Soochow on the banks of the grand canal which led into the Yangtze River. The Headquarters of The Ever Victorious Army was about thirty miles from Shanghai at Sungkiang. So long as it was under the command of Ward, its fortunes were in reasonably good health. Ward had received no professional military training, but he was an excellent leader and completely fearless. He had increased the strength of his force from one hundred ruffians to a corps of two thousand infantry and two batteries of artillery. By September of that year, he had fought seventy engagements and never been defeated. On 20 September, however, his luck ran out, and he was killed during an assault on a small town.

There were still some missionaries who believed that 'Providence [had] a wise and gracious end to serve' by the work of 'The Heavenly King'. Liberals in England dreamed of a Christian ruler, who would replace the Manchu dynasty which, times without number, had shown itself to be cruel and corrupt. As for this imagined paragon, he was comfortably installed at Nanking, no doubt taking off his mandarin's jacket to initiate his hundredth concubine in a manner which could hardly be described as evangelical.

Even the British minister in Peking, still smarting from the affront of the Taku forts incidents and the double-dealing of the dynasty, advocated a policy of non-intervention. At Shanghai, however, the businessmen were less sanguine about the Taiping ruler's mission from heaven. The British Consul suggested that the time had come to take The Ever Victorious Army in hand. Ward had been replaced by his second-in-command, H. E. Burgevine – who had shown himself to be an incompetent soldier and tactless in his dealings with the Imperial authorities. Not surprisingly, he had been dismissed. His successor had been no better. As the consul pointed out, it was foolish to attempt to replace Frederick Ward with men who were, at the best, amateurs and, at the worst dangerously bad soldiers. Couldn't General Staveley be persuaded to second one of his officers to take command? Staveley said that he had no objection, providing he had the agreement of the British government. His request for the necessary permission left at the same time as a dispatch from the minister in Peking, opposing the appointment. His Excellency's view was that the Chinese should sort out their own problems, and that the Emperor had already caused Britain sufficient trouble.

Fate sometimes moves in a most mysterious way. Staveley's note reached England without any trouble. The ship carrying the ambassador's, on the other hand, ran into a typhoon. The mail which was on board was delayed for two months – with the result that, long before the note from Peking reached Whitehall, an Order in Council had been passed. It authorized 'all military officers in Her Majesty's service to enter the service of the said Emperor'.

Staveley had already decided which of his officers to appoint. Nobody had a better understanding of the country-side than Gordon. What was more, he had the temperament which was suited to an independent command, and he had already shown ample evidence of his courage and initiative. The General approached Gordon about it two months before the Order in Council arrived, and the young officer (he was now thirty) had been enthusiastic. In late March 1863, forti-fied for his new command with the rank of brevet-major, he packed his bags and set out for Sungkiang. In a letter to his mother, he wrote:

I am afraid you will be much vexed at my having taken command of the Sungkiang force, and that I am now a mandarin. I have taken the step on consideration. I think that anyone who contributes to putting down this rebellion fulfils a humane task, and I also think tends to open China to civilization.

Mrs Gordon would have been less happy about her son's estimate of his new command. As he told a friend shortly after he had taken it over: 'I hope you do not think that I have a magnificent army. You never did see such a rabble as it was; and although I think I have improved it, it is still sadly wanting.' Nevertheless, he announced that he would free the Yangtze delta from Taiping rebels in eighteen months, and the so-called 'Garden of China' would be able to bloom again.

4
The Mandarin Years

If Englishmen at home and abroad had doubts about the wisdom of Gordon's appointment, the Chinese governor of the province most affected by the Taiping menace had no such qualms. It was just as well; for it was to him, and not to General Staveley nor to the British ambassador, that the commanding officer of The Ever Victorious Army was responsible.

Li Hung Chang, the governor, was a man with no great liking for foreigners. He found them bad mannered and conceited, and no doubt his unhappy transactions with Burgevine had strengthened these views. Nevertheless, he took to Gordon at once. 'Within two hours of his arrival,' he went on record as saying, 'he was inspecting the troops and giving orders, and I could not but rejoice at the manner in which the commands were obeyed.' He approved of the fact that this naturally irregular soldier 'did not try to impose barrack square type discipline'; and, economically, he must have applauded Gordon's attitude to finance. The Chinese were responsible for paying The Ever Victorious Army: an expenditure which cost them about £20,000 a month. Gordon's salary had been approved by Li at £3,200 a year, but the British officer had strange views on these matters. When the figure was mentioned to him, he protested that it was too much. He would prefer, he said, to receive only £1,200! Of this sum, he eventually spent four-fifths on medicine and comforts for his men. Li, who was used to dealing with more mercenary characters, was never so surprised in his life.

Gordon was faced with the immediate problems of making

an army out of a rabble. He did not impose 'barrack square type discipline', because the men would never have accepted it – and, in any case, there was not time for such niceties. Nevertheless, he realized that what they most needed was discipline. He determined to put them into what passed for uniforms; and, as an incentive to behave themselves, to substitute regular and adequate pay for the old system of allowing them to reward themselves by looting. They might be inadequate sentries at Buckingham Palace, but at least they would begin to look like soldiers.

He rode the thirty miles from Shanghai to the army's headquarters at Sungkiang on the 25 March. On the following morning, he paraded the troops; inspected them; and told them about his intentions. He also explained to them that he had no intention of dismissing anybody – and that, provided they did what they were told, he would uphold their rights. When he first appeared before them, the men were disgruntled and restless. After he had spoken to them, they seemed to be more contented. Two days later, however, they were in a dark mood once more. A local magistrate had hanged a party of them for stealing. Was Gordon going to be as good as his word? Would he really uphold them? There was little time to argue about what was right and what was not, and that their entitlements did not include a licence to rob innocent citizens. The best thing to do, he decided, was to get them out of camp and into action as quickly as possible.

According to reports, the town of Chanzu, about fifteen miles away, was being besieged by the rebels, and was on the point of surrendering. It was a strange situation, for the garrison itself was composed of former Taipings, who had become disenchanted with their leadership, and had gone over *en masse* to the Emperor's forces. When Taipings overwhelmed ex-Taipings, the result was likely to be a massacre beyond imagining. The presence of The Ever Victorious Army was needed as quickly as possible.

If Gordon had learned one lesson from the mistakes of the generals in the Crimea, it was the importance of speed. He planned to move quickly to his objective and, once there, to carry out a thorough reconnaissance. The action itself would invariably follow the lines of the battle at Tsingpu: a heavy bombardment at close range, and then a rapid assault. As time went on, and he came to understand the rebels' outlook more thoroughly, he realized that much of the fight went out of them when their line of retreat was threatened. Consequently, he deployed part of his force to threaten it. He also had the imagination to realize that an important feature of the terrain, which might seem to be an advantage to the Taipings, could equally well be turned to the benefit of his own troops. The countryside was criss-crossed by a network of canals and rivers. At first sight, these natural obstacles seemed to favour the defenders. On the other hand, provided there were sufficient boats, they could become valuable assets for transportation. After all, why go to the trouble of trying to move heavy guns over rough ground, when they could be brought into action much more quickly and easily by sending them by water? After his survey of the region, Gordon knew most of the creeks and waterways by heart. For much of its life under his command, The Ever Victorious Army resorted to a type of combined operation.

On the 31 March Gordon marched out of camp at the head of his troops. Chanzu lay just to the south of the Yangtze River, and it was obvious where the Taipings' supplies were coming from. He resolved to make the small river port of Fusan his first objective: wipe out its trade in arms and ammunition, and then double back to demolish the rebels at Chanzu. He had at his disposal a force of about 1,200 men supported by four 12-pounders and one 32-pounder. Fusan fell without any difficulty at all. Once they had been subjected to the bombardment, the rebels seemed to melt away. There were few casualties on either side. There was, however, a grim reminder of the port's past. At one of the wharves, a large freighter was rusting away. She was one of four which had been captured by the Taipings while on passage down river from Nanking. All the Europeans on board had been murdered.

Chanzu was now twelve miles away. It was a big city, built on the Muirhead Hills, which rise up suddenly from the plain to heights of about seven hundred feet, like islands in a grass green sea. Here, again, the Taipings gave in after only a brief struggle, and it was with considerably improved morale that The Ever Victorious Army marched back to its base at Sungkiang one week after it had set out. Li Hung Chang was there to greet the returning soldiers. He was in excellent spirits, and especially pleased with Gordon. Three weeks later, in a letter to the British consul at Shanghai, he wrote:

> The officer Gordon . . . having proved himself valiant, able, and honest, I have congratulated myself and memorialized his Imperial Majesty to confer on him the dignity and office of Psung-ping [Brigadier-General], to enable me to consider him as part of my command. Again, since Gordon has taken the command, he has exerted himself to organize the force, and though he had but one month he has got the force into shape . . . the people and the place are charmed with him.

On these expeditions, Gordon treated himself harshly. He seldom ate anything during the daytime, though he often made up for this lack of nourishment by consuming twelve raw eggs during the night. He slept briefly, and then usually in a couple of blankets which had been sewn together to act as a rough and ready sleeping bag. When the assault began, he was invariably the first man through the breach. He seemed to be armed only with his swagger cane, which soon became known by his soldiers as 'The Wand of Victory'. In fact, he usually had a revolver concealed under his jacket, though he used it only once in action, and that was on one of his own men who was inciting the others to mutiny. Afterwards, when the force was back at base, he made a habit of visiting wounded men in hospital. Such concern for the welfare of troops was almost unheard of in those days.

After the affair at Chanzu, Gordon busied himself with completing his reorganization of the force. Plundering, he now told the men, was forbidden. Anyone found doing it would be executed. On the other hand, to make up for the loss of this rather doubtful source of income, they would receive a rise in pay. He also took the opportunity to dismiss most of the officers – an uncertain collection of adventurers who had been recruited by Ward and, later, by Burgevine. They were to be replaced by Englishmen on loan from the garrison at Shanghai. It was hoped that they would set a better example and inject a streak of professionalism into the force. The men seemed to approve of the measure.

The strength of the force was now to be made up to four thousand – supported by four batteries of siege guns and two of fields guns. The operations against Fusan and Chanzu had confirmed Gordon's impression that the waterways would be invaluable allies to him. He now began to assemble what, for want of a more apt word, we may as well call his 'fleet'. It was comprised of a number of small steamers and Chinese gunboats, of which the most magnificent was an aged paddler named the *Hyson*. She drew only three and a half feet of water, and her design lent itself admirably to the installation of a 32-pounder gun in the bows, and a 12-pounder in the stern. Throughout the campaign, she was to be Gordon's flagship. He slept, ate, and did much of his business in the cabin which was situated just behind the funnel. The *Hyson* was a most versatile vessel, for she did not depend entirely on being afloat. If she ran aground on a mudbank, or if there was too little water in one of the creeks, she could travel on her paddle-wheels – much as if she were a steam waggon.

The relief of Chanzu had been an *ex tempore* measure, which was not carried out as part of any strategy and for which Gordon had not been certain that the troops were ready. If the Taipings had put up a strong resistance, and if their wits had not been scrambled by the artillery fire, the outcome might have been a good deal less successful. He was determined that, in future, he would not depend upon such factors. Since he was not training his men for ceremonials, he wasted no time on the parade ground. He did, however, drill them hard at attacking fortified positions. They went through it again and again – until each knew what his task was, and each reacted almost instinctively to orders. Years later, in the Second World War, the British army evolved 'battle drill'. Gordon conceived the idea way back in Sungkiang.

So far as strategy was concerned, his ideas were simple and penetrating. The Taipings would only be an effective fighting force for so long as they could get hold of supplies. They themselves were almost burning out their own revolution by creating a famine in the lands they occupied. Nevertheless, there were still overseas operators who were prepared to supply them with arms and ammunitions. For as long as the rebels commanded a sizeable stretch of the Yangtze River, this trade would continue. The operations against Fusan and Chanzu had weakened their hold in this respect. Gordon was determined to cut the lifeline completely, and the key to everything was to remove them from their base at Soochow.

The Ever Victorious Army was designed to act much in the manner of a commado striking force. Once they had captured a stronghold, the idea was to hand it over to the Imperial forces commanded by General Ching and his sidekick, who was Li Hung Chang's brother, San Tjin. They, hopefully, would secure it against any further Taiping attacks which might be mounted. Unfortunately, neither man was a very adept commander – though both had a craving for glory. While Gordon was busy training his men back at Sungkiang, San Tjin had shown an incredible naïvety by falling for a trap set by the local Taiping commander. The Chinese could be more than sufficiently obtuse when it seemed to be advantageous, and San Tjin should have been well aware of this trait among his fellow countrymen. But when, soon after the defeat of Gordon's predecessor at Taitsan, his own troops moved up to surround the town, every scrap of acumen seems to have deserted him. The local rebel commander sent him a message. He bowed before the overwhelming force of Imperial soldiers, and said that he wished to surrender. The customary gifts and vows of honour were exchanged, and it was agreed that one of the city's gates should be opened. San Tjin never questioned his adversary's good intentions. At the appointed hour, full of self-esteem at what seemed to be an easy victory, he ordered his men to march into the city. Once they were through the gate and within the walls, however, a force of Taipings rushed out of the side streets and overwhelmed them. Fifteen hundred Imperial troops were killed or captured. San Tjin managed to escape, but he was wounded. As a result of this defeat, the main Chinese army under General Ching was unable to promise Gordon any support when he was ready to resume operations.

Before an attack could be mounted against Soochow, an important outpost twenty-two miles away at Quinsan had to be captured. The city was built on the slopes of a hill, which stood up like a sugar lump above the flat landscape of the surrounding plain. It was encircled by water; and connected to Soochow by a narrow causeway, beside which lay the limpid waters of the grand canal. On either side of the causeway and canal, there were two large lakes.

A straight line is not always the quickest distance between two places – nor is it always the most feasible. Before Quinsan could be invested, Taitsan, that recurring calamity in the Imperial fortunes, had to be put out of action for once and for all. This meant that the journey to Quinsan would have to be made along two sides of a triangle, with Taitsan at the apex. How Gordon must have cursed the stupidity of San Tjin! If only the man had not underrated the determination and cunning of the Taipings, The Ever Victorious would have been saved a lot of time and trouble.

Gordon heard about the misadventure on the 27 April. By the 29th, after two forced marches, his army was outside the city. A stockade in front of one of the gates was captured without any difficulty, but then the weather turned nasty. The downpour, which lasted for two days, reduced the ground to a swamp and there could be no thought of launching an attack. However, Gordon used the enforced delay to good effect. Making use of the sparse cover, he carried out a meticulous reconnaissance. He covered a sketch pad with drawings and notes, and presently came to the conclusion that the defences were weakest at the west gate. That, then, was where he would direct the main force of his attack.

Shortly after daybreak on 1 May, he began the bombardment. Two stockades guarded the gate, and a regiment was dispatched to cut off their retreat. After twenty minutes' firing, and when they saw the troops moving into positions that threatened their rear, the rebel outposts scurried back to the comparative safety of the city. That, Gordon felt, was enough for one day. The rest of the business could wait until the fleet of gunboats, making its way slowly along the waterways, arrived. They were in position by the following morning.

The plan was an almost definitive example of Gordon's tactics. A regiment was dispatched to the north gate, to threaten what he regarded as the Taipings' most probable exit for a retreat. The gunboats, which had been brought up to within two hundred yards, blasted a breach in the walls. With Gordon leading, the first wave of attackers went in. The rebels were making a desperate stand and it seemed at first as if The Ever Victorious Army was making little progress. Then Gordon ordered the howitzers to lob shells into the centre of the city. The rear of the Taiping forces was being bombarded beyond endurance. At the same time, in their efforts to prevent the troops from coming in through the gap at the west gate, they had left another stretch of the wall unguarded. Gordon spotted this weakness. He ordered one of the regiments to leave the main assault and to scale the wall at this point. This sudden and unexpected threat to their flank was too much. The rebel opposition disintegrated. Individually and in clusters, they tried to escape from Taitsan: to fade away, as it were, into the countryside. Their casualties had been considerable, but the Ever Victorious Army had not come through unscathed. Twenty other ranks had been killed, and one hundred and forty-two wounded. One European officer had died and six of them had been wounded.

It had been a splendid victory. Taitsan the impregnable: the rebel city, which had decimated the two previous forces had fallen at last. For the moment, the men were elated. Gordon had, indeed, demonstrated his skill and courage as a commander. The pity was that the mood did not last. According to the plan, they should now be moving up on Quinsan: another brisk battle, another speedy victory, and the road to Soochow would be open. When that fell, who knew how long it would be until the rebellion was squashed for ever?

There were, however, snags. When, two days later, they came in sight of Quinsan, the city seemed to be more heavily fortified than Gordon had expected. It was surrounded by stockades and, on top of the hill, an eighteen-pounder gun was mounted. From this magnificent vantage point, it could cover all the approaches. Nor was the situation helped by the presence of General Ching, who had suddenly appeared on the scene. Ching was a braggart who saw personal glory as the beginning and the end of any military undertaking. If he had had his way outside Quinsan, the operation would have been marked by a great many deaths and precious little triumph. The only thing to do, Ching explained to Gordon, was to launch a massive frontal attack. Since they had only three thousand troops and the Taipings in the city had considerably more, the effect would have been annihilation. There were times, as Gordon took pains to point out, when it is better to fight with one's head. A little thought, a spot of imagination, and a careful survey – all these things might point to a weakness in the Taiping defences. There was bound to be one, for nothing is perfect.

Ching continued to argue; but, by now, Gordon had other things on his mind. The men were anxious to get back to Sung-kiang to spend their pay. Their growing impatience was not to be ignored and, for once, it seemed sensible to give in to them. The offensive at Taitsan had seriously depleted their stock of ammunition. With Quinsan seeming to be so strongly held, they would need fresh supplies. The operation would have to be delayed. Gordon ordered the men to return to their base:

at least it interrupted General Ching's seemingly endless talent for argument.

Back at Sungkiang, it was the officers' turn to be difficult. In an attempt to improve the efficiency and finances of the commissariat, Gordon had appointed an Englishman named Cookesley to take charge of it. It was an extremely responsible position and the entire health and welfare of The Ever Victorious Army depended on it. In recognition of this, Gordon had made Cookesley a lieutenant-colonel. This gave him the edge on the regimental commanders, who were only majors. A deputation of them went to see Gordon. If the officer in charge of the commissariat were to be a colonel, they too should be promoted. It was, after all, only fair.

Gordon could not agree with them, and he certainly did not intend that subordinate officers should tell him how to run his army. He turned the request down – whereupon, all the regimental commanders handed in their resignations. Gordon accepted them. They were no great loss anyway, and he would be happy to replace them by new blood from the British garrison at Shanghai. The dark mood spread through the ranks. If the officers went, the men said, they would refuse to march out of camp. The affairs of The Ever Victorious Army had been marked by the occasional mutiny: in this, as in deserting and even, in some instances, of going over to the enemy, the rank and file were well-practised.

In the end, Gordon had to compromise. He reinstated two of the majors, and this seemed to satisfy the other ranks. The remainder were sent packing. The army's morale began to revive, but the episode gave Gordon cause to reflect. The spectre of Ward's methods – and, more recently, Burgevine's – was all too apparent at Sungkiang. The sooner The Ever Victorious Army found itself a new base, the better it would be. When Quinsan fell, as fall it undoubtedly would, this might well be the place for it.

By 27 May, the army had left Sungkiang and was encamped near the north gate of Quinsan. Ching's flood of argument was in full spate, and Gordon must have reminded himself of the words he had written in a letter to Augusta. 'I like them [the mandarins], but they require a great deal of tact, and getting in a rage . . . is detrimental, so I put up with them.' Li Hung Chang may have helped this tolerance, for his admiration for Gordon continued unabated. Even his enemies could not have described the commander of The Ever Victorious Army as a conceited man; but Li was powerful and extremely intelligent and nearly always likeable. When he wrote that Gordon's appointment was 'a direct blessing from heaven', he no doubt meant it. It was easy to take a more gentle view of the mandarins after one had been treated to Li's blandishments.

Ching now believed that the east gate of Quinsan would be the best place for the attack. Gordon said it looked unpromising, and that he was certainly not going to commit himself to any plan until he had taken a look at the far side of the city. He proposed to use the *Hyson* for this reconnaissance, and Ching could come with him if he liked. Li Hung Chang, who had moved up to the front to observe what was obviously going to be an enthralling spectacle, said that he would go along, too.

A plan was already beginning to form in Gordon's mind. With his genius for determining an enemy's weakness, he had observed that, despite its heavy defences and the strong rebel force that manned them, Quinsan was the most vulnerable of strong-points. Its very existence depended upon supplies sent from Soochow, and its only link with the latter was the canal and the causeway. If these ribbons of communication were cut, Quinsan would fall with scarcely a fight. The idea was not to attack the city itself, but to concentrate on the stockades which defended its supply line.

The reconnaissance in the *Hyson* took them to within a thousand yards of the main canal. They could not go any further for, at this point, the creek leading into the waterway was blocked by a line of stakes. Nevertheless, with the aid of strong field glasses and perfect visibility, they could see that the junction of the creek and the canal – a village named

Chunye, eight miles from Quinsan and twelve from Soochow
– was guarded by a strong stone fort. Large numbers of troops
were seen to be moving along the causeway, and the *Hyson*'s
32-pounder let off a few rounds at them. The rebels seemed to
be taken by surprise.

Throughout the day, General Ching was, in Gordon's
words, 'sulky as a bear', and he was no better pleased when
he was told that Quinsan was not to be the main objective at
all. His dreams of glory had to evaporate, and he must have
been uncomfortably aware that he had already written a dispatch, which had been forwarded to Peking. In it, he had
claimed that he had already more or less reduced the city,
and that he only needed a boat to move into it. However,
there was no denying the sense of Gordon's arguments; the
Chinese commander had to be content to grumble.

At dawn on the following day, Gordon's fleet set off.

> The whole flotilla [he wrote] some eighty boats, with their
> large white sails, and decorated with the usual amount of
> various-coloured flags, with the *Hyson* in the middle, pre-
> sented a very picturesque sight, and must have made the
> garrison of Quinsan feel uncomfortable, as they could see
> the smallest move from the high hill inside the city, and
> knew, of course, more than we did of the importance of
> the stockades about to be attacked.

By noon, they had reached the line of stakes that had halted
the *Hyson*'s progress on the previous day. The crews of a small
force of Imperial gunboats, which had departed a few hours
earlier, pulled them up, and the last physical obstacle before
the main canal was removed. The rebels, who seemed to be
thrown into panic by the approaching armada, fled from the
nearest stockades. When, shortly afterwards, the *Hyson*
steamed into the canal, other members of the opposition
scattered. Some fled towards Quinsan. Others hurried off in the
direction of Soochow. The 4th Regiment of The Ever Victorious Army, which was four hundred strong and was accompanied by field-artillery, was told to go after those who sought

sanctuary in Quinsan. The *Hyson* would take the left hand turn, and travel away from the city – towards Soochow.

The paddle steamer had to proceed slowly. There were innumerable boats, which had been abandoned by their owners and were now clogging the waterway. The enemy seemed to be completely demoralized: the *Hyson* had only six Europeans and thirty Chinamen on board, yet she encountered no opposition at all. The rebels simply fled – encouraged now and again by a burst of gunfire from the steamer. The forts along the causeway were abandoned and, in most cases, the Taipings had left their weapons behind. It was all almost laughably easy. On one occasion, Gordon went ashore to rescue a naked baby from the scrimmage of departing rebels. He named the child Quincey (the nearest he could get to the name 'Quinsan'). The child was later educated at Gordon's expense, and rose to become chief of the Shanghai-Nanking railway police.

At another time, the master of the *Hyson*, a Captain Davidson, ran his vessel into the bank. A party of soldiers stepped ashore and without any difficulty captured a hundred and fifty Taiping troops. Later, a rebel leader, who was galloping towards Soochow, fell off his horse and into the canal. He managed to clamber ashore, but he had to make the rest of the journey on foot. Crowds of villagers, who seemed to spring up from nowhere, obligingly set fire to the rebels' forts at Gordon's request. Then they helped themselves from the collection of unattended boats which were drifting around.

The experience was intoxicating. Li Hung Chang was in raptures, and afterwards wrote: 'What a sight for tired eyes and elixir for a heavy heart it is to see this splendid Englishman fight!' There had, admittedly, been very little combat so far, but an easy victory is hardly less satisfying than one which has been achieved with bloodshed and difficulty.

At six o'clock in the afternoon, when they were only a mile from Soochow, Gordon decided that the picnic had gone on for long enough. There were still plenty of Taipings in Quinsan, and they might have manned the fortifications to the

Hyson's rear. The steamer was turned round, and they headed back.

When they were within two hundred yards of Quinsan, Gordon saw 'a confused mass near a high bridge. It was too dark to distinguish very clearly; but on the steamer blowing her whistle, the mass wavered, yelled, and turned in its tracks; it was the garrison of Quinsan attempting to escape to Soochow – some seven or eight thousand men'.

What, under these circumstances, should a commander do? Throughout the day, Gordon had been merciful: only firing when the occasion insisted on it, and then mostly to give the fleeing rebels a prod. The present situation, however, was more serious. He wrote: 'Matters were in too critical a state to hesitate, as the mass of rebels, goaded into desperation, would have swept our small force away. We were therefore forced to fire into them.'

When it was all over, it was estimated that the rebels had lost between three and four thousand killed, drowned, or taken prisoner. The Ever Victorious Army helped itself to eight hundred of the captives, most of whom promptly threw off their allegiance to the Taipings, and enlisted in its ranks. Gordon's own casualties that day had been negligible. The strong outpost of the enemy had fallen because he had discovered its weak point. It was a victory for intelligence rather than a triumph of arms.

The next objective was obviously Soochow; but, before that could be attacked, there was the problem of transferring the headquarters of The Ever Victorious Army from Sungkiang to Quinsan. Quite apart from the fact that it would enable Gordon to remove his command from the ghost of Ward, it was a sensible thing to do; for it commanded one of the approaches to Soochow, and the army's communications would become less stretched when the time came to attack the city. The trouble was that The Ever Victorious Army didn't wish the move to take place. Some of them lived in Sungkiang, most of them had friends or mistresses in the town. It was a reminder of the gay old days, when there had been booty to dispose of, and discipline had been very much more lax.

Led by their NCOs, the gunners mutinied. Gordon quelled the insurrection by ordering the leader to be shot on the spot. Afterwards, two thousand soldiers deserted, but there were plenty of Taiping prisoners who were only too willing to serve on what was obviously (in their estimation) going to be the winning side. Manpower, indeed, now became the least of his problems.

General Ching, still brooding over what he considered to be his humiliation over the capture of Quinsan, caused a party of his troops to fire on a column of Gordon's men. Gordon was so furious, that he would have attacked Ching's troops. Luckily for everyone concerned, the incident was cooled down by the intervention of Li Hung Chang's personal secretary, an engaging Scottish doctor named Halliday Macartney.

Everything seemed to be conspiring to make life difficult for Gordon. Some of the English language newspapers were accusing The Ever Victorious Army of committing atrocities. There was not the slightest evidence to show that they had done any such thing, but this did not stop the articulate do-gooders from raising their usually anonymous voices. Even the Bishop of Australia, from his sacred perch at least one thousand miles away, chimed in. All of them seemed to be unaware that a large area of China, including Shanghai – where the garrison had now been run down until it was only a token force – depended on Gordon and his men for their well-being, their wealth, and their lives.

Even Gordon's devoted friend and admirer, Li Hung Chang, was acting strangely by suddenly withholding funds with which to pay the troops. Eventually, Gordon became so fed-up with the whole tiresome business, that he resigned. He still believed that the cause was a good one, and that the Chinese people's only hope for the future lay in overcoming the Tai-pings. But there were limits to what a man could stand. Eventually, the matter came to the attention of the British consul in Shanghai, who brought pressure on Li to pay up, and then turned his persuasion on Gordon. As he told him, there was 'no other officer who combined so many dashing qualities, let alone skill and judgement'. This was all very nice, but the factor which did most to influence Gordon's change of mind was the news that Burgevine had gone over to the enemy. Burgevine is memorable for his ability to fail at whatever he attempted. He had been briefly in command of The Ever Victorious Army, but Li Hung sacked him for his hot-tempered incompetence. Immediately after his dismissal, he hurried off to Peking in an attempt to be reinstated. The authorities were unimpressed. Burgevine skulked back to Shanghai, where he set himself up in business trading arms to the Taipings. He then conceived the idea of raising a force to fight with the rebels.

Alas – nothing went right for this arch-blunderer. His intentions were no doubt those of a villain: his performance was that of a clown. He was arrested outside rebel territory, and Gordon, no less, had to bail him out. Once he was free, he scampered down to Sungkiang for what he assured his bene-factor would be profitable talks. Gordon was away when he arrived. Instead of waiting patiently. Burgevine seized a river steamer named the *Kajow*, and sailed away to what he hoped would be a triumphant reception by the Taipings.

He was to be disappointed. The rebels had a far greater regard for their enemy, Gordon, than they had for this untrust-worthy and, possibly, reluctant ally. In a desperate bid to improve his image, Burgevine then suggested that he should kidnap Gordon, and hand him over to them. The Taiping leaders had the sense to see that this was not even an opium pipe dream. Nevertheless, he attempted to enlist the help of the *Kajow*'s master. The worthy seaman turned him down, for he, too, was an admirer of Gordon. In a fit of pique, Burgevine attempted to murder him, but he even mismanaged that. All that he could now do was to throw himself on Gordon's mercy. As he rightly assumed, his life was no longer worth much among the rebels in Soochow.

Meanwhile, the long, hot, Chinese summer dragged on. Back in July, Gordon, who was in frequent correspondence with the Taiping leaders, suggested that they should surrender. They were still in a position to bargain, and they might expect to be offered reasonable terms by the Emperor. However, this situation would not last for very much longer. They'd be wise to cut their losses. The rebels thanked him for the idea, but declined it. The war would have to continue, and this meant that Soochow would have to fall.

Encouraged by the success of his methods at Quinsan, Gordon decided at first to employ a similar technique against this next objective.

The rebels are working hard upon the defences of Soochow, [he wrote] a place I have no idea of attacking. I hope (DV) to cut off both the main roads, and to isolate the town by so doing. This would make it only a matter of time as to its fall. With the small force one has at one's command, I am not anxious to pit myself against a town garrisoned by seven, or even ten times our numbers, if it can be avoided.

In spite of all the demands on his attention – the troubles with his own troops, the bickering with Li over pay, and the duplicity of Burgevine – Gordon had managed to keep operations going. By the 24 August, he had invested Soochow on the eastern and southern sides. But the political in-fighting continued. One leading Chinese statesman, who had heard about the trouble with Li, suggested that Gordon should apply to Peking for an independent commission.

Of course, the Futai [Li Hung Chang's Chinese title] is happy to find place after place fall before you; but you may be sure he'll take most of the credit to himself . . . Therefore, you ought to be appointed from headquarters. In the Futai's employ, notwithstanding your commission under imperial edict, you stand on unsafe ground. Although the Futai speaks and writes well of you, he looks upon you as a temporary evil, necessary, perhaps, under the circumstances, but to be got rid of as soon as things change.

But Gordon was tired of intrigue. He was a simple soldier, who only wanted to carry out his duties – which, in this instance, were the overthrow of the Taipings. If only the politicians would keep their opinions to themselves, and let him get on with it! He was a man whose trade was battle, murder and sudden death. True to his religious leanings, he went into an action praying, and his prayers lasted until the end of it. But they were not for his own safety, nor for the rewards of success. All that he asked of the Almighty was that he should be allowed to win, and that his troops would not run away. It may seem a little unfair to ask God to take sides, but there are few commanders who have not made similar requests. Victory, after all, is a soldier's merchandise.

Burgevine's treachery at Sungkiang had been a bad blow to Gordon. It was not the loss of the *Kajow* that he minded so much as the fact that he had stood surety for the American. In his mind, he transferred Burgevine's guilt to himself; and it was this which, finally, made him withdraw his resignation. His one consolation was that the man was such an inadequate commander. 'There is no knowing,' he wrote, 'what an immense amount of damage might have been done if the rebels had had a more energetic man than Burgevine.' In the end, he forgave him. When at last, Burgevine decided that he could no longer endure life in Soochow, it was Gordon who negotiated his surrender – and Gordon who saw that he received a safe-conduct pass back to Shanghai. Afterwards the American consul there wrote to thank him for 'his great kindness to the misguided General [sic] Burgevine and his men'. But the act was typical of him.

During the investiture of Soochow, one of his own officers, a Captain Perry, had been discovered selling information to the enemy. He was brought before Gordon, who was understandably very vexed indeed. However, he was prepared to overlook the matter on one condition. During the next difficult engagement, Perry should lead the assault on the stockades. It can hardly be regarded as a sentence of death, for Gordon himself was constantly running with his head thrust forward

71

through a hail of enemy bullets. By the time the occasion
arose, he had forgotten all about the matter; but Perry, who
seems to have been a more honourable man than his trans-
action with the Taipings might suggest, had remembered. He
led the charge as he had contracted. A bullet hit him in the
mouth, and he literally fell into Gordon's arms. He was the
first man to die in that particular battle. When it was over,
Gordon told everybody that he was 'a very good officer'.

The Chinese used to say that 'if Paradise is in heaven, there
is Soochow on earth'. It was, indeed, a most beautiful city.
A grey stone wall, the design interrupted from time to time by
small turrets, surrounded it. Above the wall, innumerable
pagodas craned their necks into the sky, rising, it seemed out
of an ocean of trees of every conceivable kind. Here and there,
the shimmering roof of a palace appeared. In front of the city,
a contemporary observer wrote,

> the proximity of the rebel line became apparent with sur-
> prising suddenness, for, following their usual custom, they
> greeted the rising sun with a simultaneous display of gaudy
> banners above the line of their entrenchments. The mud
> walls they had thrown up, scarcely distinguishable before,
> were now marked out by thousands of flags of every colour
> from black to crimson, whilst behind them rose the jangling
> roll of gongs, and the murmurs of an invisible multitude.

To hold this delightful place, which was also a strongpoint
of enormous importance, the supreme commander of the
Taiping forces, Chung Wang, had a force of about eighteen
thousand troops. The opposing army, which now included The
Ever Victorious, a large corps of the Imperial army, and
another detachment of irregulars which had been trained by
the French and were commanded by French officers, amounted
to about twenty thousand. The overthrow of the city should
have been easy, but the Chinese were playing politics again.
General Ching was feuding with San Tjin, which was hardly
surprising, for the two men disliked each other at the best

of times. Now, with the prospect of the spoils of victory and a mammoth reputation to be won, they were going at it hammer and tongs. Gordon was reluctant to leave Ching to his own devices, for he was bound to do something stupid. And, on top of all this, Li Hung Chang arrived – no doubt to ensure that he, too, received fair recognition for the triumph. It was an operation in which, it sometimes seemed, there were more soldiers spectating than there were taking part in the fighting.

The Ever Victorious Army was systematically taking town after town, stockade after stockade, as it closed in on the city. Once again, Gordon's method was seen to be the right one. 'The great thing in taking stockades from the rebels,' he wrote, 'is to cut off their retreat, and the chances are they will go without trouble; but attack them in front, and leave their retreat open, and they will fight most desperately.' By the end of November, most of the fight had gone out of the Taipings, and the city fell with very little opposition. As Gordon observed: 'We had expected a most desperate defence. If ever men deserved beheading, the Taiping leaders did on this occasion.'

In fact, the Taiping leaders were disagreeing among themselves. When, on 29 November, the siege guns began a bombardment, a party of them were deciding what to do next. At some point in the discussion, Chung Wang rode into town, escorted by a bodyguard of a few hundred men. He brought the argument to a swift conclusion, and suggested that, rather than discuss surrender terms, they might be better employed in trying to hold the city.

But the days of rebel successes were long past. Soochow was obviously about to be overwhelmed. The negotiations for surrender had already begun by the 4 December, when the Taiping leaders came together for a banquet at the palace of Mow Wang. Mow Wang was the man who had rejected Burgevine's overtures: he was a good soldier and a man whom Gordon greatly respected. Of all the rebels, he was now the only one who wanted to make a last desperate stand.

During the meal, he stood up to make a speech. He told

73

his colleagues that he did not think Li Hung Chang was to be trusted, and they would do better to fight on. This was dangerous talk – although, as it transpired, he was right. But he was not allowed to finish. Before he had completed his argument, he was murdered. His head, it was said, was sent to Li as a gesture of good faith. The members of his thirty-man body-guard were slaughtered at the same time.

Throughout the surrender transactions, Gordon's role was thoroughly scrupulous. He insisted that there should be no reprisals: that, whatever terms were finally agreed upon, Li should spare the rebel leaders' lives. The governor promised him that this would be done. When, at last, the main gate was opened, Gordon ordered his soldiers to remain behind their stockades. Let loose in Soochow, they would have gone mad. The men obeyed, though with a bad grace. However, he promised them that he would persuade Li to award them two months' extra pay – as a reward for their victory and as a compensation for their lack of loot. They seemed to be satisfied.

Unfortunately, Li Hung Chang was still being difficult. Why two months? he asked. The Imperial forces of Ching were only being offered one month's. That, surely, was enough. Gordon was furious. When he told the men about it, they reacted in much the manner he had expected – to such an extent that he was compelled to put a guard on the governor's boat. On the following day, 6 December, he marched them back to Quinsan. Nobody was sorry to see The Ever Victorious Army depart. Their successes had shown up the weak and incompetent leadership of the Imperial troops. Now, with them out of the way, the generals could glory in the triumph which was not of their making.

But Gordon was uneasy about the situation in Soochow. Once he had seen his troops back to camp, he hurriedly returned to the city. There was an invitation waiting for him from Li. The surrender ceremony was to be carried out that night on board his boat. There was to be a banquet, and Gordon's presence was requested. He declined. It may have been that he was still angry with the governor, though it seems more likely that he wanted to spare the feelings of the rebel leaders. If he were there, it might seem to be flaunting his successes against them. He preferred to keep out of the way. Presumably, he still felt sure that Li, whatever his faults might be, would remain true to their agreement, and that the Taiping commanders would not be killed.

There was nothing much to be done. Soochow had occupied much of his thoughts and most of his activities for the past few months. Now that his work was over, at any rate for the time being, he might as well see something of the city. Gordon the tourist took over in spite of the fact that he was desperately tired. During the last days of the siege, he had never undressed and had seldom slept at all. As soon as the *Hyson* arrived, he proposed to get a good night's sleep, but the steamer was still on passage. He had several hours to kill, and how better to pass them than to explore this Chinese paradise on earth.

Accompanied by a youth who acted as interpreter, he set off. As he passed through the gates, the Taiping leaders rode by on their way to Li's boat. They were laughing, and they seemed to be unarmed. On the other hand, they had not shaved their heads, which was the traditional Chinese way of signifying surrender. But Gordon thought nothing of it. Perhaps that would come later.

While he was exploring the streets, he met Dr Macartney, who joined him. They strolled to the eastern wall, which overlooked Li's headquarters. There seemed to be an unusually large crowd there but, again, Gordon thought nothing of it. He was more perturbed when, shortly afterwards, a party of Imperial troops rode into the city. They were firing their guns and shouting, and he protested to the officer in charge of them. Since Soochow was still crowded with rebels, such an attitude was, surely, asking for trouble. At this point, General Ching arrived. He had imagined that Gordon was on board his steamer – chasing the *Kajow* up the lake. He looked worried when he saw him. Gordon asked how the surrender was going, and Ching muttered something about one of the rebel leaders, Lar Wang, making unreasonable demands. He had, he said, walked out of the meeting and had, presumably, returned to his palace. When Ching moved off on his tour of inspection, Gordon asked Macartney to go to Lar Wang's palace, and reassure him.

Gordon continued his walk. It is obvious that any semblance of order in Soochow was rapidly breaking up. Imperialist troops were pillaging the palaces, and groups of angry Taipings were roaming the streets. Whenever he asked his interpreter for an explanation, the answer was always evasive. At last, by now worried about the situation, he decided to make his own way to Lar Wang's palace. Macartney had already left. There was no sign of the leader, the place had been gutted by the Imperialists, and there was only a very anxious elder relative, who begged Gordon to take the womenfolk to his house for safety. Within a few seconds of his arrival there, the courtyard was suddenly invaded by a force of Taipings, who barricaded the gates, and refused to allow him to leave.

It was now midnight. The Imperial troops were trying to force their way into the house, and the Taipings were preparing to repel them. At last, when things had quietened down a bit, Gordon's captors agreed that the interpreter should be allowed to summon his bodyguard – on the understanding that the youth was escorted by two Taipings, and that he should also send a detachment of troops to seize Li Hung Chang, who was to be held as hostage for the lives of the rebel leaders. Gordon agreed. On the way, however, the three men were attacked by a squad of Imperialists, who wounded the interpreter and tore up the instructions. When news of this reached the house, Gordon was at last permitted to go. On his way to the city gate, he, too, was arrested by the Imperialists. The men had failed to recognize him, and it was not until well into the morning that he was at last able to make his way to the east gate. Ching was waiting there. Gordon was furious. The take-over of Soochow had been carried out abominably. There was murder and chaos everywhere. He had the most grave doubts about whether Li had been true to his undertaking: would Ching kindly tell him whether the rebel leaders were alive or dead? Ching hedged. He bent before the storm of Gordon's rage and, as the latter noted, 'made a precipitate retreat into the city'.

Presently one of Gordon's English officers arrived. He had a message from Ching to the effect that the Chinese general didn't know what had become of the leaders. But, he said, he had Lar Wang's son in his tent. Would Gordon like to see him? Gordon replied that he most certainly would, and the boy was brought before him. He was obviously very distressed. His father, he said, had been executed on the other side of the creek.

At about this time, another Ever Victorious Army officer named Prince von Wittgenstein turned up. Gordon asked him to take a boat and row across the creek as quickly as possible to see what had happened. The prince returned immediately. He had, he said, seen nine headless bodies. It later transpired that the leaders had never gone to Li's boat. Shortly after Gordon has passed them at the gate, they had been met by General Ching, who had escorted them to a stockade. Li had received them: there had been a brief conversation, and then the governor had departed. A squad of Imperial troops had then closed the stockade gates. The soldiers seized the leaders – and beheaded them.

Gordon arranged for the corpses to be buried before, at last, he went on board the *Hyson* – taking Lar Wang's son with him. He told Captain Davidson to make for Quinsan along the canal. He then retired to his cabin in a mood in which anger and despair were evenly mixed, and in which hatred of Li Hung Chang for his double dealing was only matched by his contempt for himself at having trusted the man. There was also a feeling, somewhere at the back of his mind, that Li had not only been deceitful, but also incredibly foolish. If reasonable terms had been offered and honoured, the Taiping rebellion would have been ended by the fall of Soochow. As things were, the rebels would have no alternative but to fight to the last round. In a box beneath his bed lay Lar Wang's head, which he had taken from Soochow as a fearful reminder of the betrayal of the rebel leaders and, he believed, of himself.

5

The Return of the Soldier

The taking of Soochow should have been the ecstasy of Gordon's career in China. Instead, it was the agony. Later on, he was to be wounded in an engagement; but the injury was less painful, the shock nothing to the suffering which the massacre of the Taiping leaders caused him. He had taken two souvenirs from the city. One was the head of Lar Wang. The other was the sword of Chung Wang, which had been given to the Taiping general by 'The King of Heaven' himself. It was a magnificent object, more ornament than weapon, covered by a yellow silk case embroidered with dragons. The general had escaped from Soochow: in his hurried departure, he had left it behind in one of the palaces. When he looked at the head, Gordon saw Li Hung Chang's perfidy. When he studied the sword, he observed his stupidity. Chung Wang, the most formidable of the Taiping leaders, lived to fight another day – and, in view of what had passed, he most certainly would fight.

Gordon had offered China everything, including his life. In some ways the situation resembled Vietnam. It was somebody else's war; the leaders on both sides were a lot less than admirable; and in all the negotiations which took place, there was a great deal of double talk. Why, then, did Gordon commit himself so completely? The survey, which General Staveley had ordered, had convinced him of the wrongness of the Taiping rule. Throughout the campaign, his letters home insisted that he was fighting for the starving peasants, and not for the businessmen and rulers. Once he had taken this line, his professional pride became involved. He was one of nature's heroes, the very stuff of which early *Boy's Own Paper* characters were made. Although Gordon disliked publicity, he had a talent for drama, and he displayed it whenever he led The Ever Victorious Army into battle. It was the secret of his leadership: the reason why his polyglot collection of irregular troops maintained such discipline in the face of the enemy.

His drama now was to be with Lar Wang's head in the loneliness of his cabin, dead tired, and yet unable to sleep – his mind a tangled pattern of plans to avenge the execution of the Soochow rebel princes. It was still morning, though so much time seemed to have passed that he was almost unaware of the difference between day and night. Presently, he sat down at his desk and wrote a letter to the governor. He remarked bitterly on what had taken place, and demanded Li's resignation. If Li did not comply immediately, he would turn The Ever Victorious Army against the Imperial forces, and recapture all the places that he had taken from the Taipings. He would then return them to the rebels as a gesture of contrition. It was, perhaps, a foolish document, for it greatly exceeded his authority. But that was how he felt: if necessary, he would take Li himself into custody as soon as his force of gunboats had been reassembled.

The letter was intercepted by Dr Halliday Macartney. Once he had read the first paragraph or two, he realized that it was diplomatic dynamite, and he refused to translate the rest of it. However, Li had learned enough about Gordon's frame of mind, and he ordered Macartney to proceed as fast as possible to Quinsan on a peace-making mission. The doctor commandeered a boat with a team of Chinese oarsmen, and set off down the canal. It was late at night – how many nights had passed since the murder of the Wangs? It seemed like an eternity – when he came alongside the *Hyson*. He was told that Gordon was in bed, and was, on no account, to be disturbed. His servant made Macartney some coffee, and the doctor sat in the saloon to wait for daybreak.

Shortly before dawn, there were noises from Gordon's room. Presently the servant came into the saloon, and said that his master was now available. Macartney went into his cabin where, in the pale early morning light, he saw Gordon sitting on his bed. Suddenly he reached underneath it and drew out Lar Wang's head. 'Do you see that?' he asked. 'It is the head of Lar Wang, foully murdered.' Then he burst into tears.

There was nothing to say. Macartney walked to the door, and said that he would see Gordon later.

Some hours later, breakfast was served. As well as the officers of The Ever Victorious Army, there were a number of Shanghai traders present; men who were responsible for sending supplies to the army's commissariat. When Gordon came in, Macartney sat down beside him. There was an ominous silence. Then, suddenly, Gordon turned and barked: 'You have not come for yourself. You have come on a mission from the Futai. What is it?'

Macartney said that it might, perhaps, be better to talk about the matter in private. Gordon looked round the room. 'There are only friends here,' he said, 'I have no secrets. Speak out.' There was nothing else for it: Macartney passed on a message from Li to the effect that he took complete responsibility for the massacre, and that Gordon was in no way implicated. 'This,' he told him, 'is China – not Europe!' Different standards applied, and it had not been easy to show the rebel leaders mercy. Gordon had seen them – they had not shaved their heads to signify surrender. As for Gordon's letter to Li,

it was [he said] a great mistake.... A little reflection will show you that, to carry on a personal war with the Futai, would be to undo all the good you have done. Moreover, you must recollect that although you, no doubt, have at this moment the military force to carry out your threats, it will no longer be paid for by the Chinese authorities. You will only be able to keep your men at your back by allowing them to plunder, and how long will that prove successful, and what credit will you get by it?

Gordon replied that he'd have none of the Scotsman's 'mild counsels'. He ordered the engineer of the *Hyson* to raise steam, and a platoon of infantry to stand by. They were going back to Soochow to take Li Hung Chang prisoner. Macartney could come along too, if he wished.

The envoy's answer was to borrow a horse and a pair of spurs from one of the officers, and to ride off to Li Hung Chang's headquarters as fast as he could. Fortunately, after he had gone, Gordon did pause to reflect. He began to accept the fact that China was not a country in which he could expect the laws of western chivalry to be observed. His very individual brand of religious fatalism also came to his aid. 'My only consolation,' he wrote some while later, 'was that everything is for the best.' Even, he might have added, when it appears to be for the worse.

For the next few weeks, he and The Ever Victorious Army waited at Quinsan for instructions. After several previous efforts had failed, Li's attempts to make peace with Gordon reached a climax on New Year's Day, 1864. Gordon first became aware that something was in the wind, when a senior Chinese officer arrived at his quarters. He had been ordered to bring Major Gordon an Imperial decree and gifts from Peking as a reward for his share in the capture of Soochow. Gordon said that he wanted nothing whatever to do with it. The officer told him that he could refuse the gifts if he liked; but that he might, at least, have the courtesy to receive the mandarin who was acting as the Emperor's emissary. A procession was waiting at the west gate of the city. Would he be so good as to go there? Grudgingly, Gordon agreed. He met the mandarin, and saw that he was accompanied by bearers carrying the sum of 10,000 taels (about £3,000) in caskets. There were also four banners – two of them were Li's, the others had been captured from the Taipings.

Gordon rejected Li Hung Chang's banners and all of the cash. Even if it had not been connected in his mind with the shameful episode of the murdered rebels, he would not have accepted it. He wanted no rewards and his dislike of money, which almost amounted to a phobia, compelled him to turn down all gifts of this nature. On the back of the Emperor's manuscript, he hurriedly wrote:

> Major Gordon receives the approbation of His Majesty the Emperor with every gratification, but regrets most sincerely that owing to circumstances which occurred since the capture of Soochow, he is unable to receive any mark of His Majesty the Emperor's recognition, and therefore respectfully begs His Majesty to receive his thanks for the intended kindness, and to allow him to decline the same.

And there matters had to rest for another month. He had already resigned from his post and was no longer, technically at any rate, in command of The Ever Victorious Army. Indeed, inactivity and uncertainty had reduced the morale of that force to a very low ebb and the other ranks were once again on the verge of mutiny. It was this, probably more than anything else, which caused him to patch up his relations with Li Hung Chang. As a professional soldier, he hated to see a body of men, whom he had drilled into a wonderfully efficient war machine, gradually going to pieces. It made all his work, all his inspiration, seem pointless. The Taipings had not been completely conquered. The Ever Victorious Army, back on its own form, could complete the operation in a few months. Without them, it was impossible to say how long it would take. As one Englishman (Sir Robert Hart) who was attached to the Chinese government observed: 'The destiny of China is at the present moment in the hands of Gordon more than of any other man.' Moreover, Li Hung Chang had at last resolved to take action which would assuage Gordon's anger. He agreed to pay the troops their bounty of two months' extra pay – he was even willing to give an extra sum to the wounded by way of compensation. On 18 February, The Ever Victorious Army marched out of Quinsan towards the next battlefield. Gordon, who had been promoted to lieutenant-colonel on the previous day, was at the head of the leading column.

The territory still held by the rebels was shaped rather like an hour-glass, with Nanking at the northern end, and Hangchow at the southern. Yesing and Liyang were situated opposite each other at the waist. Once they were captured, the Taiping forces would be split in two. The Ever Victorious Army would then deal with the rebels to the north, whilst the Franco-Chinese irregulars would mop up the strongholds in the south. Yesing was taken by surprise, and, on the 1 March, the enemy capitulated with scarcely a shot being fired. The enemy themselves assisted in the capture of Liyang by disagreeing with one another. Half of the fifteen-thousand-strong garrison wished to surrender, whilst the other half was in favour of holding out. Fortunately, the former prevailed. Gordon guaranteed their personal safety, and the city was taken without any casualties at all. It was just as well that the Taipings had decided to give in, for the place was heavily fortified and had enough provisions to withstand a siege lasting several months. The food was distributed to the local peasants, who had been enduring the inevitable famine which attended Taiping rule. Since many of them, in desperation, had been living off human flesh, it made a pleasant change. Two thousand five hundred of the prisoners were enlisted into The Ever Victorious Army; and, all in all, it had been a most satisfactory day's work.

From Liyang, the army marched northwards to Kintang where the rebels put up an unusually desperate fight and things were not going well for The Ever Victorious Army. Gordon was wounded in the leg, but had recovered sufficiently to order a fresh attack when a messenger arrived from Li Hung Chang. It seemed that Chung Wang, with a master stroke of strategy, had decided to resume the offensive against the Imperial troops at a point as far away as possible from Gordon. He had selected the Yangtze port of Fusan, which was held by that eager fool of a general, San Tjin. San Tjin allowed Chung to turn his flank: the rebels recaptured the town, and then moved south west to lay seige to Chanzu.

Gordon was far from well. An Imperial edict, no less,

ordered Li to call on him daily, and asked him to postpone future operations 'until he shall be perfectly restored to health and strength'. But The Ever Victorious Army without him was no army at all. It lost cohesion, and the other officers, no matter how valiant they might be, seemed incapable of fighting with their brains. Gordon's wound put him out of action for two weeks. In one of the engagements during this period – an attempt to clear up the situation around Fusan and Chanzu – the men suffered their only major defeat since he had taken over. The initial advance by the infantry was made without any covering fire from the gunboats. Nevertheless, it was partially successful, and the officers became careless. When the Taipings counter-attacked, one of the crack rifle regiments suddenly became overcome by panic and fled. The men were pursued for three miles by a squadron of rebel cavalry. Seven officers and more than two hundred and fifty men were killed. It was the darkest day in the life of The Ever Victorious since Gordon had taken it over.

Fortunately Gordon recovered in time to prevent any more disasters. The towns were re-taken. Chung's headquarters at Waissoo was overwhelmed, and ten thousand rebels fled. Only half of this number ever reached safety. The remainder were butchered by the peasants who, when the foe was unarmed, were much more ruthless than Gordon's men. Years of hardship, hunger, and senseless killing by the Taipings, had filled their minds with a fearful lust for revenge. It was small wonder that many of the defeated rebels were eager to join Gordon's ranks. Whatever the perils of combat, they were safer there than they would otherwise have been.

The Ever Victorious Army, which was now working with the Imperial troops, fought its last engagement at Chanchufu on the grand canal, where Chung Wang was determined to make a last, desperate, stand. The garrison was manned by twenty thousand crack Taiping troops, who had already been besieged for several weeks. Working at night, Gordon directed the digging of a system of trenches, which would take the men under cover to the walls of the city. During the daytime, large posters were put up, offering terms to any of the rebels who cared to surrender. At last, on the 11 May, the preparations were complete. At midday, the combined force went into the assault. The trench system enabled the bulk of the troops to get through the breach without any casualties, though Gordon himself had a near miss. He was running over the skyline, when he found himself face-to-face with the business end of the Taipings' 32-pounder. For a second or two, it looked as if his moment of triumph would also be his moment of death. But he was still indestructable. The gun would not fire. He marched coolly into the city. Soon afterwards, the battle was won. Chung Wang fled to Nanking: the days of the Taiping were almost over.

Gordon had a considerable admiration for the general. He was, he wrote,

the bravest, most talented, and enterprising leader the rebels had. He had been in more engagements than any other rebel leader, and could always be distinguished. His presence with the Taipings was equal to a reinforcement of 5,000 men, and was always felt by the superior way in which the rebels resisted.

When Nanking finally fell to the Imperial troops, Chung was sentenced to be executed. The beheading was, however, postponed for long enough to allow him time to write his memoirs. After the victory, Gordon wrote a letter to his mother.

Chanchufu was carried by assault by the Quinsan Force and Imperialists at 2 p.m. this day with little loss. I go back to Quinsan on the 13th May, and shall not again take the field. The Rebels are now done, they have only Tayan and Nanking, and the former will fall probably in a day or two, and Nanking in about two months. I am happy to say I got off safe.

Chanchufu had fallen on the 11th. On the 13th, as Gordon had foreseen, his army marched back to Quinsan to be disbanded. It had been arranged that his contract with the

Chinese should come to an end on 1 June. In spite of his eagerness to get back to England, this date was extended. Li wanted him to raise and train a Chinese force with skills similar to those of The Ever Victorious Army. He also paid a visit to the Imperialist forces, which were investing Nanking. That city fell on 19 July. The final act of the Taiping rebellion was performed by The King of Heaven himself. He had lived like an emperor, and he was determined to die like one. In the traditional Imperial manner, he committed suicide by eating a quantity of gold leaf.

Gordon wanted no lavish farewells from The Ever Victorious Army, which was obediently going into liquidation. Most of the men had been offered re-employment by Li Hung Chang, and he had managed to persuade Li to pay them generous grants. As for himself: 'I know I shall leave China as poor as I entered it,' he wrote, 'but with the knowledge that, through my weak instrumentality, upwards of eighty to one hundred thousand lives have been spared. I want no further satisfaction than this.'

The fact that he was not to benefit financially was entirely his own doing. The Emperor had offered him a large sum of money after the fall of Soochow, and he was anxious to do so now. But such an act would have been useless – Gordon was bound to turn it down. On the other hand, if he would not accept wealth, he could not refuse honour. He was made a field marshal in the Chinese army – with all the trappings of dress which went with the appointment. When he unpacked the exquisite robes, the peacock feathers, and the yellow jackets, his comment was, perhaps, typical. He observed that 'some of the buttons on the mandarin hats are worth thirty or forty pounds. I am sorry for it, as they cannot afford it over well; it is, at any rate, very civil of them.' He was certainly proud to receive the yellow jacket which denoted a mandarin, and which only fifty or sixty men were entitled to wear. He was no less pleased with the two gold medals, which the Emperor had ordered to be struck in his honour. The British government was less generous. They confined their recognition of his work to awarding him the Companionship of the Bath – an honour which any reasonably industrious civil servant might hope to earn.

One evening, towards the end of November, Gordon departed quietly from Quinsan in the *Hyson* on the first stage of his journey home. He had hoped to avoid any demonstrations; but, as the paddle steamer set off down river, the banks were thronged with soldiers, who saluted him with gunfire, crackers, and a tumult of gongs and horns and anything else which would make a noise. They waved their flags and lanterns in affectionate farewell, and Gordon waved gently in return. Even he, who mistrusted and fought shy of displays of this kind, could not be unmoved by the troops' spontaneous exhibition of love for their departing leader.

At Shanghai, the business leaders presented him with an eulogy with fifty-five signatures on it. It rolled out such ponderous phrases as 'Your career during the last two years of your residence in the East has been, so far as we know, without a parallel in the history of the intercourse of foreign nations with China.' And:

> in a position of unequalled difficulty, and surrounded by complications of every possible nature, you have succeeded in offering to the eyes of the Chinese nation, no less by your loyal and, throughout, disinterested line of action, than by your conspicuous gallantry and talent for organization and command, the example of a foreign officer serving the Government of his country with honourable fidelity and undeviating self-respect.

And so on, and so forth. As a maze of prose, it was scarcely less complicated than the network of Chinese waters he knew so well. One suspects that Gordon, who succeeded in compressing an account of The Ever Victorious Army on to five sheets of paper, without once mentioning his own name, preferred the final salute of his own men.

He now only wanted to go home – and with as little fuss as possible. As he had written earlier to his mother: 'The individual is coming home, but does not wish it known, for it would be a signal for the disbanded to come to Southampton, and although the waits at Christmas are bad, these others are worse.' He had, indeed, gone to unusual lengths to become inconspicuous. Before leaving Quinsan, he had ordered a suit from Shanghai. He detested new clothes, and this outfit looked altogether too smart. Consequently, when he set off in the *Hyson*, the steamer had a strange cargo trailing astern of her. It was the suit, crammed into a bowler hat, being subjected to the muddy waters in an attempt to make it look well worn.

Chinese Gordon sailed in the P & O boat from Shanghai in a blaze of glory. He was determined that, by the time he reached home, it should have burnt itself out. He was, above all things, a very modest man.

PART II

The Administrator

6
The Errands of Mercy

Lieutenant-Colonel Charles Gordon arrived at Southampton in January 1865. He was wearing the bowler hat and suit he had bought in Shanghai. His mandarin's outfit had been carefully packed in a trunk; otherwise, he had little in the way of personal baggage. When he had left England some four and a half years previously, he had been an anonymous young officer in the Royal Engineers. Now, at the age of thirty-three, he was a celebrity. People called him 'Chinese Gordon': they were eager to hear his account of the adventures against the Taipings. He must, they all agreed, have some very remarkable stories to relate. The trouble was that Gordon did not wish to tell them. He wanted nothing of the fame which was now thrust upon him: he only asked that he should be allowed to fade silently into the background.

It was a difficult home-coming. His family was now living at Rockstone Place, Southampton. They were, not unnaturally, anxious to make the most of their hero. Similarly, almost every post seemed to bring him an invitation to this or that reception. Some were from private admirers, others were official. Few of them ever received a reply. The authorities gradually came to the conclusion that here was a very strange bird indeed. If he had remained in China, he could have helped himself to almost any position he chose. He was, after all, a field marshal in that country's army, and one of the nation's elite of sixty or so mandarins. Instead, he preferred to ignore this opportunity for power and wealth: to slink quietly away the moment his work was done.

The situation in Britain was not entirely different. He was

famous: if he did the right things, acted the part of a celebrity, went to the correct parties, enthralled influential people who were only too eager to hear his stories, he could have received considerable preferment. Instead, he did his best to cut himself off completely. The Establishment branded him as eccentric. The invitations gradually ceased. The important jobs were given to other people: the man who had shown himself to be a past master of irregular warfare was overlooked. Although, by a strange quirk of the times, his army rank was that of lieutenant-colonel, within the Royal Engineers he was still only a captain. The corps's insistence that promotion should only be achieved by seniority was inflexible. It mattered not that one of their officers had distinguished himself on a foreign field with an army of men who were little better than bandits.

He was entitled to two years' leave, but it seemed unlikely that he could endure so much leisure. He was as energetic and impulsive as ever, and he must have found the atmosphere at Rockstone Place stifling. His father's health was failing, and he was to die before the year was out. His mother was, as a mother would be, anxious to show him off. Sister Augusta was possessive and tyrannical. At family prayers, it was she who read the Lord's Prayer, while the others meekly observed a pious silence. When brother Charles joined in fortissimo, there was some anxiety about how Augusta would react. Happily, she said nothing – though she may have flashed him a look in which surprise and disapproval were combined.

Visitors who were invited by Mrs Gordon to the house, and who hoped to hear about the exploits of the famous son, went away disappointed. The famous son said nothing. Once, when he found his mother proudly exhibiting a map which he had made when a cadet at the Royal Military Academy, he snatched it away from her, and threw it into the grate. Luckily, since there was no fire burning, it was presently rescued. The journal of his operations against the Taipings was less fortunate. In a moment of anxiety that it might be used to advance his fame, he destroyed it. It was, perhaps, a foolish gesture, for it was obviously a document of considerable historical importance.

Occasionally, when the family was alone, he broke his silence and told them stories about the campaign. But these sudden outbursts of communication would only endure for so long as his listeners curbed their very natural instinct to admire him. Approval was acceptable: anything beyond that would cause him to become silent – even, sometimes, to stalk out of the room.

No doubt some of the reason for this apparent bashfulness was the fact that he was tired. For the past two years, he had been living under a considerable strain and in a great deal of danger. Whatever successes he had achieved with The Ever Victorious Army had been marred by the fate of the rebel leaders at Soochow. He had been one of the men who had guaranteed their lives in return for the surrender of the city. Despite what Li Hung Chang may have said, he felt responsible for their fate. The Chinese may have broken their promise: that did not matter. *His* promise had been broken, and the shame still haunted him. He was, furthermore, shy. He was afraid of his quick outbursts of rage, and he found it almost impossible to be tactful. If good manners or expediency suggested that he should say something which was untrue, he could not bring himself to utter it. As in warfare, his approach to conversation was often uncomfortably direct. One can see him searching for the weak point in somebody's argument: the sudden barrage and then the assault. He was often an uncomfortable companion, and he knew it. It was better to remain silent.

Perhaps his curious and often intense relationship with God gave him all the company he required. At all events, he was a solitary. In China, his only close friend had been The Ever Victorious Army's surgeon, a Dr Moffit who later married his sister Helen. Otherwise, he kept himself apart. In moments of extreme stress, he preferred to be alone: confiding, no doubt, to the Almighty doubts and fears which he would not dream of discussing with anyone of a less transcendental character.

The days and weeks at Rockstone Place dragged by. He resolutely refused, as he put it, to 'board the tram of the world' – in other words, to grab the power and applause which might have been his. The world, the life, and the body were passing things of only small importance. Salvation and the glorious coming to eternity were what mattered. All else was vanity. That was what he believed – at any rate for most of the time. There were, however, lapses, which showed that he was not quite so completely prepared to sacrifice the opportunities of today for the promise of an everlasting tomorrow. Two years after he had returned home from China, for example, the King of Abyssinia had seized and imprisoned all the British subjects in his country. The War Office arranged an expeditionary force to rescue them. As Gordon was only too well aware, he was the natural person to take charge of it. His experiences in China had fitted him for precisely this type of irregular warfare. But, no! The task was given to the Indian army, and Sir Robert Napier was appointed to command it. Napier was, in any case, Gordon's senior by twenty-five years. Even so, when he heard about it, Gordon was so upset that he retreated to his quarters for two days, and refused to see anybody.

Meanwhile, at Southampton, he did his best to play the role of dutiful son. He accompanied his mother on drives, and served, he said, as her *'Aide de Camp'*. He discussed theology with Augusta: trying, all the time, to conceal his restlessness. He refused an invitation from his friend Major John Donnelly to visit the Paris Exhibition ('I do so cordially hate anything of the sort proposed, that I would go anywhere to avoid them'); and, presently, let it be known to the Royal Engineers that he would happily forego the rest of his leave – if they could give him something to do. As it happened, they did have a job for him, though it seems a strange appointment for a man of Gordon's proven ability in other directions, and in the light of his often stated preference for service overseas.

On 1 September 1865, a mere eight months after his return to England, he was appointed Chief Royal Engineer at Gravesend.

Here Gordon was given the unenviable work of supervising the completion of a series of forts along the Thames. These were intended to serve as a protection against French invasion, but they were so poorly designed and badly positioned as to be virtually useless. Every instinct of this inspired tactician must have rebelled against the project. The politicians, in their ignorance, might imagine that it was work of strategic importance. The Chief Royal Engineer, on the other hand, could see all too uncomfortably that it was sheer folly – and a terrible waste of public money, which might have been more effectively spent on much more urgent social projects. With an uncharacteristic resignation, he moved into his headquarters at a large, timbered, vaguely Tudor-looking building named Fort House (adjacent to the New Tavern Fort at Gravesend), and settled down for six years which were to be at once the worst and the best of his life.

As the contractors charged with the construction of the forts quickly found out, Gordon had lost none of his energy and impatience. Arthur Stannard, who was assistant manager of the firm, was impressed as soon as he met him for the first time. 'The next moment,' he recalled, 'I was looking into Chinese Gordon's eyes. What eyes they were! Keen and clear, filled with the beauty of holiness, bright with an unnatural brightness, their expression one of unsettled feverishness.' It may seem to be pretty high-flown language for a man in the building trade, but there is no reason to doubt its authenticity.

Gordon's working day began at 8 a.m. and finished at 2 p.m. Everything about it seemed to be directed at getting the work done as quickly as possible – though it is doubtful whether this was with an eye to completing the construction of the forts, or to freeing himself for other activities. The former assignment was certainly the least urgent of any he ever undertook, but he tackled it in a mood of infinite impatience. When a boat rowed by two oars seemed to be too slow for his journeys up and down river, he replaced it by one with four oars; and, even then, he was merciless in his demands on the men who rowed it. 'A little faster, boys, a little faster,' he continually urged them. Often, the wretched watermen finished their day's work in a state of utter exhaustion.

When he toured the construction projects, he moved at a brisk pace which was almost as much a run as a walk. The unfortunate supervisors followed breathlessly behind him, knowing that he would spot the smallest fault. When the men seemed to be working too slowly, he would point out that 'another five minutes gone – and this not done, my men! We shall never have them again.' Even when he took his lunch, he refused to relax. He invariably ate at his desk, which was fitted with a deep drawer. If anybody came into the room, he hastily put the food into it – to give the impression that the caller was not disturbing him. It was hardly worth hiding. He had already conceived a belief, which recurred throughout his career, that he was suffering from *angina pectoris*. Since he was his own doctor as was he his own priest, he prescribed his own cure. Semi-starvation he believed was the answer, and so, except when he was entertaining, he ate frugally. His love of raw eggs, which was such a standby in China, remained. During the night, he would often visit the larder and eat a dozen of them.

After two o'clock in the afternoon, he was free to live his other life, which was a mixture of spiritual devotion and practical Christianity. According to one of the sapper officers, he was 'the nearest approach to Jesus Christ of any man who ever lived'. The claim is a substantial one, though there was much to justify it. In Gravesend, as in most parts of Britain at that time, there was a great deal of poverty. Foremost among the victims were the children: ragged, half-starved, uneducated creatures, whose present plight seemed to be as hopeless as their future expectations. If his work for the army was, in the final analysis, contributing to a monumental waste of money, his work for the poor of Gravesend was positive and effective. He began by taking in two or three of these waifs. He fed and

clothed them, and in the evenings, taught them. Before long
the population of Fort House had grown considerably, and
there was as many as a dozen small boys in residence. The
class grew, until it became too big for one room; and it was
not, simply, the promise of clothes and a square meal which
attracted the pupils. Gordon may have been shy with grown-
ups, but all his reserve fell away with these children. He was
that rarest of beings – a natural teacher. Pupils who had
attended the local charity school noticed, at once, that this
was someone different. They had been used to the lifeless
routine, the attempts to batter knowledge into unreceptive
minds, which has always been the mainstay of the men and
women who undertake this ill-paid and often thankless profession. But Gordon was no hack teacher: no disillusioned
educationalist who is used to blank stares in return for threats
and uninspiring torrents of supposedly important knowledge.
He told them stories; he spiced his instruction with humour;
he somehow infected them with his own enthusiasm. He seems
to have found it easy to enter into their minds, and he was
never given to those fits of irritation which often characterized
his relations with grown-ups. As a relic of his days in China,
he called the boys his 'Wangs' (Kings) and this may have been
his secret. He gave them two things which most of them had
never had before – and would never have dared hope for:
affection and a sense of personal pride. To Gordon, these dirty
scraps of humanity were important, and, therefore, they
discovered resources in themselves which they had never suspected existed.

Gordon was never a wealthy man, and there is no indication that, at this stage in his career, he had anything more
than his army pay to live on. Nevertheless, he spent a great
deal of money on these boys. He bought them boots by the
gross and suits by the score. Sometimes, he sat up all night
mending their clothes (a closely guarded secret: if people
found out, they might commit the unpardonable offence of
admiring him). When they were old enough, and were able
to face the world with some chances of success, he found them

jobs. Although he was a bad sailor, he had a great liking for the sea. Consequently, most of the positions were on board ship. At one time, he had a large map of the world on the wall of his office. The positions of various vessels in which a 'Wang' was serving were marked by flags. He became a sort of information centre for the boys' relatives. When a ship with one of these lads in her crew arrived in the London River, it was an occasion for much rejoicing at Fort House.

Sometimes, there were failures. One boy, who had been given the Gordon treatment and sent out into the world, was discovered, some while later, clad in rags and covered in vermin. He was brought back to Fort House, where Gordon received him. It was late at night. The boy was given bread and a mug of milk, and a bed of fresh straw in the stable. At six o'clock on the following morning, Gordon woke him up. He, personally, stripped him of his rags, washed him down in the horse trough, and redressed him in a new suit. Adults, especially those in his profession, had to abide by harsher standards. These boys were permitted to fail. Another lad, who had been rescued from the gutter in a sick and starving condition, was rehabilitated and sent back to his parents in Norfolk. Gordon never heard from him again – there were no progress reports and no letter of thanks. Some, on the other hand, did well for themselves. Shortly after Gordon's death at Khartoum, his brother Henry received a visitor. Was there, the man wondered, going to be a memorial erected? If so, he would like to contribute £25 towards it. He was, he explained, one of the Gravesend 'Wangs'. He had made a success of his life, and this, he insisted, had been entirely due to the good fortune which had taken him to Fort House.

Throughout his life, Gordon did a great deal to help boys and youths. This, plus the fact that he never married and sometimes seemed to dislike women, was the reason why, in later years, some people suggested that he might have been a homosexual. There is no more evidence to support this view than there is to substantiate Margot Asquith's suggestion that

'Gordon was a confirmed opium eater, and consequently often muddled, although always a great or rare man' – or the view, reflected in Lytton Strachey's *Eminent Victorians*, that he was an alcoholic. In later life, at the time he was telling people that he had gone to the Crimean War in the hope of being killed, he also professed that, at the age of fourteen, he had wished to be a eunuch. Did he have some unsavoury experience when he was at school at Taunton? It is possible: homosexuality was rife in Victorian boarding schools, though it was not until the trial of Oscar Wilde that anybody seemed prepared to acknowledge its existence. If this, in fact, did happen, his short-lived adolescent ambition can only be taken as evidence of his shame. It was calculated to stifle, rather than to encourage any such trait in his character.

As for his relationship with women, he was dominated (so far as he was dominated by anybody) by that arch-dragon, Augusta. When his younger brother, Freddy, married a girl named Frances, Gordon did not take kindly to the match. He had not liked her, for he observed that she had 'a hard-looking jaw, which promises a very acidulated old age'. In this respect, she probably resembled the jealous and possessive Augusta. One liked having Augusta as a sister – but, as Gordon must surely have acknowledged, she would have made an uncommonly uncomfortable wife. If his sister-in-law's jaw was hard, Augusta's was pure granite.

Even so, he often advocated marriage for other people. 'A man who is not married cannot know his faults,' he once wrote. 'A man's wife is his faithful looking glass.' And: 'To marry is the best thing a man should do, and it is one which I recommend to all my friends.' But, not for himself. 'I could make no woman happy,' he noted, and he knew himself sufficiently well to be sure of this. Nobody – not even Augusta, to whom he wrote most of his letters – really knew Gordon. What seems most likely is that he always kept something back in his personal relationships: that there was a part of himself he was prepared to surrender to God, but to no one else. He had the sense to see that a successful marriage is an act of total surrender, the crossing of a boundary beyond which he was not prepared to go. Since he was not interested in doing anything less than perfectly, and because he may have realized that he was incapable of love for an individual, he wisely kept away from women. In any case, it was just as well. His taste for living rough, preferably in some remote corner of the world, was scarcely calculated to achieve domestic bliss. Maintaining his status as a confirmed bachelor was no doubt the kindest thing he could do for the opposite sex.

At Gravesend, there was plenty to engage his attentions. He may not have been able to offer much to women of his own class, but there was a lot that he could do for the impoverished, the sick and the dying – and this was by no means confined to his 'wangs' (or, to employ a Mancunian word he sometimes used, his 'scuttlers'). Fort House had a large and pleasantly shaded garden. Gordon, himself, was not an enthusiastic gardener: he preferred, he said, to 'look at human faces'. Nevertheless, it was well stocked with flowers and vegetables, and a number of the aged and the infirm of Gravesend were given keys to it. They were, he assured them, cordially invited to spend as much of their time as they liked there.

Nearly all his leisure – or such of it as was left over after his attentions to the 'wangs' – was spent at the bedsides of the sick. He read the Bible to them; he talked to them; and he was a particular comfort to those who were dying. It may have been that they found the tone of his gentle, almost tender, voice soothing. Very likely they were encouraged by his own certainty of a future life, and one which was very much happier than the present. At all events, parish priests of all denominations used to call him in on these occasions.

He appears to have seen himself as an unhappy, almost tragic, figure. Once, when reading a description of Byron in one of Murray's International Guides, he remarked that he 'was a melancholy and unhappy man, and I am no better'. He decided that this gave him an affinity with the poor. It is difficult to see what produced this streak of almost morbid sadness, though it may have been that this world compared so unfavourably with his picture of the next. Certainly, if his letters to Augusta were anything to go by, he was in a great hurry to get there. One December, he wrote to her: 'I must write and wish you a happy Christmas. I will not say many of them, for our joy is in our Lord, and we cannot wish many years will pass before He comes to deliver us from our contemptible bodies and infirmities.'

He seemed to have a longing for death. For example, after a visit to the forts, his gig hit an obstruction as it came alongside the jetty. The small craft filled with water and sank, but the calamity was not serious. Gordon waded ashore with no difficulty. Later, however, he regretted that the accident had not occurred in mid-stream. Then, he would have been drowned, and he would have attained 'the very bright, happy land with beautiful sights and glories'.

The key to his religious life was what he called 'the secret', and he came across it by chance. One evening, he was dressing for dinner, when his eye happened to alight on a Bible which lay on the table. He focused on the following sentence: 'Whosoever confesseth that Jesus is the Son of God, God dwelleth in him and he in God.' Gordon was not above adapting extracts from the good book fairly freely when it suited his purpose, and he frequently misquoted. He never belonged to any particular sect: his religion was more or less manufactured by himself. Once he had found 'the secret', everything else stemmed from it.

A man who knows not the secret, [he told Augusta] who has not the indwelling of God revealed to him . . . takes the promises and curses as addressed to him as one man, and will not hear of there being any birth before his natural birth, in any existence except with the body he is in. The man to whom the secret (i.e., the indwelling) is revealed . . . applies the promises to one and the curses to the other . . . he then sees he is not of this world, for when he speaks of

103

himself, he quite disregards the body his soul lives in, which is earthly.

He wore his body as he might a suit of clothes. Like the suit, it was disposable. Just as he had spoilt the outfit he bought in Shanghai by dragging it through the muddy waters of a river, so was he prepared to humiliate his own flesh.

Although he referred to it as 'the secret', it was something that he was only too eager to share with other people. He had dozens of tracts printed. He threw them out of railway carriage windows; handed them, on impulse, to strangers in the street; some he left behind in what seemed to be appropriate places. For instance, after he had been for a walk in the country, people were liable to find one of these brief messages held down by a stone on a stile. It would say, 'Take heed that thou stumbleth not.'

His demand for these leaflets brought him into contact with a couple named Freese. Mr Freese, whose health was bad, had founded the Gravesend branch of the Religious Tract Society. He and his wife lived near Fort House, and Ada Freese recalled their first meeting. He was 'almost boyish in his appearance and in *some* of his utterances, yet with an eye and an expression that might have lived 1,000 years – I felt that he was no ordinary man.' Neither she nor her husband knew that he was *Chinese* Gordon; for when, later on, he was invited to tea, he happened to mention that country. In all innocence, Mr Freese asked him whether he had been there.

The Freeses helped Gordon in his charitable works, and so did the local Presbyterian minister, a Mr Lilley, who became his unpaid assistant. There were visits to hospitals, workhouses, and schools. Those who passed on were helped by the comforting words of the Colonel (the 'wangs' called him the 'Kernel'); those who survived to face an old age of poverty, were helped by him, too. At one time, he was paying about £300 a year in pensions to old and disabled people. A visit to the north brought a sudden realization of the poverty which the cotton famine, caused by the American Civil War, had produced. Something ought to be done about it. Gordon's answer was to throw his most precious possession into the poor box. It was the gold medal presented to him by the Chinese Emperor. He had removed the inscription, but the parting was none the less painful. For years afterwards, he used to say 'You must give up your medal,' when urging somebody to carry out an act of self-sacrifice.

Now and then, he slipped up to London to the Junior United Services Club; and, on one evening, he was taken to see *The Pirates of Penzance* at the Savoy Theatre. He seems to have enjoyed it, though he was almost as tone deaf as he was colour blind. It was just as well. There was, he said, too much misery in the world for it to be right to attend concerts. He read a great deal: newspapers, translations of the classics, Thomas à Kempis's *The Imitation of Christ*, and, of course, the Bible. In the afternoons, he used to like to walk across the fields to the church at Chalk – leaving a paper trail of tracts in his wake. He took tea frequently at the Freeses, where Ada Freese became almost as much a sounding board for his religious theories as Augusta was.

Occasionally, he went back to Southampton on leave. Once, just before Christmas, he had to make a sudden change to his plans, for one of the 'wangs' went down with typhus. He spent the holidays nursing the boy. At Rockstone Place, Gordon's father had died in September 1865, at the age of sixty. His mother was now becoming querulous with age. She grumbled when he was out of her sight; and, though he would never have admitted it, it must have been something of a relief to return to Fort House and the less demanding 'wangs'. He had been compelled to sell his horse to raise funds for his innumerable charities; but he had the services of a house-keeper, whom he affectionately nicknamed 'The Giantess' (one has to assume that it referred to the magnitude of her spirit in coping with the demands of her philanthropic master). The ducks in the garden were named after royalty. Once, when Gordon put aside his image as a melancholy figure, haunted by the sins of the world and by the burden of the flesh, he described this period as 'the most peaceful and happy of any portion of my life'. He may have been right. Whatever his letters to Augusta may have suggested, he was often in high spirits. One suspects that, if this phase of his career had been allowed to continue, he might have achieved something spectacular. In 1908, Lord Baden-Powell founded the Boy Scout movement. It does not require a large stretch of the imagination to see that Gordon might have created something similar. No matter whether with his 'wangs' or with his irregular forces, he was a kind of super scoutmaster.

But, a long way from Gravesend the world was moving uneasily about its business. Grateful for the diversion of the Franco-Prussian war, the Russians were doing their best to tear up quietly all the conditions of the Treaty of Paris, which had ended the Crimean war. The naval base at Sebastapol was being rebuilt; the mouth of the Danube was becoming closed to navigation; the Turks were stirring uneasily – pushing, one might say, a round up the breech, and pointing the rifle at the Russians. In a word, the Near East was in its customary mess.

The time had come for Gordon to move. The British membership of the Danubian Commission had become vacant. Gordon was known to prefer overseas service: he had worked on the frontier question after the Crimean War, and the people at the Horse Guards believed they might be doing him a good turn by giving him the job. The object was to open the Danube for navigation once more – though the Foreign Office suggested that it was certainly not an exacting, and not really an important, appointment. Bending gracefully before what he assumed to be the will of God, and what was most certainly the will of the War Office, Gordon packed his bags. On 1 October 1871 he sailed for Galatz (Galati), a small Rumanian town on the Danube.

Galatz was ghastly. Gordon's salary was £2,000 a year; and, to his way of thinking, he earned every penny of it. Some people may have enjoyed the claustrophic social atmosphere: the parties; the polite smiles which looked as if they had been wrought from wax; the endless niggling of very minor diplomats; and the job itself, which was to ensure that dredgers scooped out a sufficiency of mud to enable ships to sail from the Black Sea into the belly of Europe. The officials at the Horse Guards no doubt meant well, when they posted Gordon to this place: but, to condemn a man of his type to this hothouse of intrigue and smallness, was not far short of brutal. The only diversions were trips to Bulgaria, where Gordon the Tourist explored the countryside – and a visit to the graveyards in the Crimea, and to Constantinople, where Gordon the Soldier advised: 'Have nothing to do with the Turk. I know him well, he is hopeless.'

Back in England, his mother died in 1872, after a distressing illness in which, towards the end, she was unable to recognize him. His brother, Freddy, passed away soon afterwards – leaving the hard-jawed Frances, six children, and very little money. Freddy's widow, he wrote home later, when he was serving in Equatoria, should be given every opportunity to marry again, 'if there is any chance of such a thing. If I live and can stay out another six months, to let her have another £1,000 of her own, beyond the £2,000 for the children, I would do so if it would make her more marketable.'* He was, for the record, still paying out £250 a year in pensions for the poor at Gravesend. There was, it seemed, no limit to the demands on his munificence.

It was during a visit to Constantinople that Gordon first met an Egyptian diplomat named Nubar Pasha. Nubar told him that Sir Samuel Baker, governor of the Khedive's Equatorial provinces, was about to retire. They were looking for a replacement. Would, he wondered, Gordon be interested? Gordon was vague in his reply. Indeed, he had almost for-

---

* He was, perhaps, rather hard on his sister-in-law. He implies that he was making sacrifices to support her and the children – although, during the period in question, he had insisted on receiving only one-fifth of the salary he had been offered.

gotten about the incident when, a year later, he received a telegram. It confirmed that Sir Samuel was giving up his duties, and offered him the appointment at £10,000 a year.

Gordon hesitated. He wrote to the adjutant general and discovered that neither the War Office nor the government would object to his accepting. He then read up a great deal about the Khedive, Baker, and the darker part of darkest Africa; hesitated some more; and finally decided to accept the post – though not, he insisted, at £10,000 a year. Two thousand a year was what he had received in Galatz: it would be quite sufficient for the new job. When his assistant, Mr Lilley, had found himself in financial trouble at Gravesend, Gordon wrote to him that 'you and I will never learn wisdom in money matters.' Certainly, when asking him to accept a job, the problem was not to decide how much to pay him, but how little.

By 1 November 1873, his successor at Galatz had been appointed, and he was on his way back to England via Berlin. He took home with him few favourable memories of the place. The best thing had probably been a reunion with an Italian named Romolo Gessi. They had first met when Gessi had been serving as an interpreter in the Crimea. Now, he was running a Rumanian saw-mill within easy reach of Gordon's residence. The two men got on excellently together, and one of Gordon's earliest actions, once he had decided to take the Equatorial job, was to invite the Italian to join his staff. Gessi, in spite of fierce opposition from his wife, accepted. Between them, they had one of the hardest assignments in the world: to wipe out the slave trade in Africa. If, hitherto, Gordon had been looking for something which really stretched his capabilities, he had found it at last. In January 1874, he set off for Alexandria on what was obviously going to be a very long journey. When, later in the month, he arrived at Cairo, the first person to meet him was Romolo Gessi.

7

The Dark Journey

During one of his more melancholy moments in the African jungle, Gordon gave vent to his disillusionment over his recent appointment. He had, he observed, 'thought the thing would be real and found it a sham, and felt like a Gordon who has been humbugged.' His disenchantment was not without cause. The Egyptian officials, whose rule rolled along the length of the Nile with ever diminishing effectiveness, were as slippery a bunch of men as ever tried to play cops and robbers simultaneously. As for their soldiers: they were useless. A handful of fit natives, armed with spears, were more than a match for a company of them – Remington rifles and all. They had neither the skill nor moral fibre – and, worst of all, they lacked leadership.

But why, it might be asked, did Gordon go to Equatoria in the first place? It was certainly not for the money, and there must have been something more positive than, simply, getting away from Galatz. In a letter to Augusta – which, like many of them, was really an attempt to self-analyse – he wrote: 'The thing slid on little by little. I felt too independent to serve, with my views, at Malta, or in the corps, and perhaps I felt I had in me something that, if God willed, might benefit these lands, for He has given me great energy and health, and some little common sense.'

These lands certainly needed benefiting. In 1819, Egypt had conquered the Sudan. The capital, which had been at a place named Shendi, was shifted to Khartoum on the left bank of the Blue Nile three miles south of its junction with the White Nile. It consisted of three thousand mud huts, a number of houses

– mostly owned by wealthy Egyptians – and the governor's residence, which was somewhat euphemistically known as 'The Palace'. The building was heavily fortified. One side of it was situated on the Blue Nile. A moat protected the other walls; and a gun, mounted on the flat roof, commanded both rivers.

In 1853, the Egyptians pushed their outposts forward to one hundred and twenty miles south of Khartoum, but this was only the beginning. Where the Egyptian authorities stopped, the European traders went on. The ivory trade was profitable enough; but these men, a number of Englishmen among them, found something which paid even better. The commodity was known as 'black ivory' – or, to put it more bluntly – slaves. The wealthy Turks, whose homes were scattered throughout the Near East had an almost insatiable appetite for these items of human merchandise. Entire villages became depopulated, until things reached such a point that there was a counter-blast of criticism. The Europeans – all of whom had, no doubt, been richly rewarded by the slave network – knew when to stop. They sold their stations to Arab agents who, hitherto, had acted as go-betweens. Then they pulled out. But this did not mean that the slave trade was over. The Europeans might have surrendered to public (mainly European) opinion, but the Arabs cared nothing for it. They traded on, throwing a pall of misery wider, until any native living in the Sudan regarded each day of freedom as a bounty.

The area from which people could be pillaged was considerable. On the east, it extended down the Red Sea to Abyssinia. In the west, it encompassed Darfur, which bulged out towards French Equatorial Africa; and it stretched out southwards, through sweltering jungle, until it halted at the frontier with Uganda. The dealers watched their profits grow. Any threat to their commercial future was easily avoided by passing on a scrap of largesse to the ever-extended palm of authority.

But the slave traders were becoming too powerful for the Khedive of Egypt's liking. One of them, in particular, disturbed him: a flamboyant brute of a man named Zebehr

Rahama, whose escort included a no longer quite so proud pride of chained lions, and whose armoury was enriched by twenty-five thousand dollars' worth of silver bullets – to fire, it must be assumed, at enemies who were proof against the more commonplace variety. Zebehr had built himself a slave empire in the south of Darfur at Bahr el Ghazal, and he now felt sufficiently strong to refuse the Egyptian authorities their customary bribes. This, in the opinion of the Khedive, was going too far. In 1869, he sent an expeditionary force into Bahr el Ghazal with the intention of reducing the villain to a state of suitable submission. The slave dealer watched with amusement. His forces annihilated the Khedive's army, and they did not even bother to use silver bullets. Zebehr was now, to all intents and purposes, dictator of all the Sudan south of Khartoum.

Sir Samuel Baker had made his first visit to the Equatorial provinces in 1864. He returned in 1869 to take up the duties of governor-general with a particular responsibility for wiping out the slave trade.

It is [he wrote] impossible to describe the change that has taken place since I last visited this country. It was then a perfect garden, thickly populated, and producing all that man could desire. The villages were numerous, groves of plantains fringed the steep cliffs on the river's bank, and the natives were neatly dressed in the bark cloth of the country. The scene has changed! All is wilderness. The population has fled! This is the certain result of the settlement of Khartoum traders. They kidnap the women and children for slaves, and plunder and destroy wherever they set their foot.

The assignment turned out to be too much for Baker, who presently resigned – with, it was alleged, a golden handshake of £20,000. It was left to Gordon to clear up the mess – if, indeed, it could ever be cleared up.

Gordon's charter, as explained to him by Khedive Ismail, was the same as Baker's. He was to subjugate the country to the south of the farthest-flung Egyptian outpost at Gondokoro; suppress the slave business; introduce a system of regular commerce; and open up a trade route from the great lakes of Albert and Victoria. These two inland seas had been discovered fourteen years previously, and they were regarded, almost literally, as the heart of Africa. Once the forces which they seemed to represent had been released, all manner of projects would become possible. Who knows – the continent might one day become a commercial rival to Europe (but, hopefully, with Europeans in financial control, and thereby making sure that the indigenous population was not excessively rewarded by its rich heritage).

Gordon arrived in Cairo on 7 February 1874. He spent two weeks in the city, talking things over with the Khedive, and assembling his staff. During his encounters with the former, he quickly came to realize that, if he and Mr Lilley would never learn wisdom in money matters, the Egyptian ruler was even more financially naïve. He and his country were living entirely on borrowed cash – and at what a price! As Gordon noticed with a sense of shock, he was paying no less than thirty-six per cent interest on some of the loans.

It was pointed out that – officially at any rate – Gordon would come under the governor-general of the Sudan, a gentleman named Ismail Ayoub Pasha. His administrative headquarters would be at Gondokoro a place about which nobody, wisely as it turned out, had troubled to find out very much. The Khedive made haste to explain the economic importance of the work. Darfur alone was costing him £50,000 a year, and the only person who benefited from it was that scoundrel Zebehr. If Gordon could wring some profit out of Equatoria, it would be much to His Highness's liking. The people at Gondokoro would be informed that he was coming. That was all. Good luck.

Gordon set about recruiting his staff. There was Romolo Gessi, who, since his work in the Crimea, had distinguished himself with Garibaldi – he was essential. A Frenchman named Linant offered to join as interpreter, and two young

Gordon in the trenches before Sebastopol, 1885

Storming Soochow, November 1863

Gordon in Chinese costume

The house which Gordon occupied at Gravesend

Teaching the ' wangs ' at Gravesend, 1867

A last goodbye: Gordon leaving Charing Cross on his final mission to the Sudan, January 1884

Opposite: Khartoum as it was during the siege
Key: A the Austrian mission convent ;   B garden of the Austrian mission ;   C the palace (Gordon's headquarters) ;   D government buildings ;   E barracks ;   F Tuti ;   G Omdurman ;   H fortified camp, Omdurman ;   J the White Nile ;   K the Blue Nile

Gordon's last stand

A contemporary
cartoon depicting
Gladstone's failure to
save Gordon: 'Tommy
Atkins mounted on
Too Late by Verbosity
out of Vacillation'

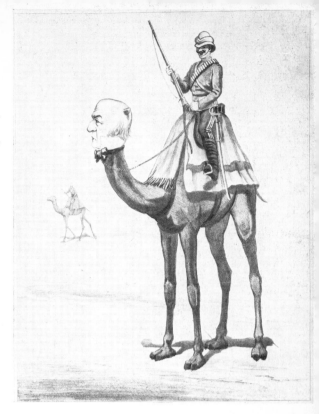

A terrible
trophy: Gordon's
head is brought
to Slatin Pasha

The Governor-General of Khartoum as he will be remembered

German botanists asked whether they could come along. They volunteered to act as Gordon's servants. There were four Englishmen – including Gordon's nephew Anson, and an engineer named Kemp. Back in China, some of The Ever Victorious Army's best troops had been Taipings who had come over from the rebel ranks. They were not only good fighters: they brought with them priceless information. What was more, they helped Gordon to put himself into the mind of the enemy. He now determined that his mission would benefit, if he had a former slave trader in his ranks. He found just such a person in Abou Said, who was currently serving a sentence in the Cairo gaol. He was deceitful, a liar, thoroughly corrupt, and nobody had a good word to say for him. Nevertheless Gordon had a hunch about the man. He decided to ask for his release and appoint him as his lieutenant. 'All the people are dead against Abou Said,' he wrote, 'but I am faithful to him, and trust to a higher power to bring me through.' The higher power seldom refused Gordon reasonable requests, but this was unreasonable. What is more, if Gordon flourished from Abou Said's successes, the Arab would prosper, too. That was surely too much to ask. Abou Said's nest egg of divine credit had become dangerously low.

They left Cairo by train on 21 February, travelling by steamer to Suakim and thence to Berber by camel, a form of transport which was entirely new to Gordon and which proved to suit him admirably.

From Berber, the last leg of their journey to Khartoum was by river steamer. They reached the Sudanese capital on 13 March, and picked up two hundred and fifty troops, another aide (a toady of the governor-general named Raouf Pasha), and some good news. The thousand miles of river up to Gondokoro were clear. They would be able to reach their destination by mid-April. If the stream had been blocked, as it frequently was, it would have taken them anything from eighteen months to two years.

As they steamed away through the desert to the south of

H 113

Khartoum, there were four vessels in the convoy. The voyage was to take them twenty-one days. They churned on towards the destination. The river became fringed with broad tracts of marshland. Forests of tall reeds seemed to close in on them: the fierce heat of the desert became more humid. It was a heavy, listless feeling – like the sweat of a fever. It seemed as if a tangible thing called strength was pouring away with the perspiration which seeped from their skins. 'No one can conceive the utter misery of these lands,' Gordon wrote, 'heat and mosquitoes day and night, all the year round.' They passed an island in the river, which had once been an Austrian missionary station, but the priests had long since abandoned it. Of the twenty men who had worked there, fifteen lay buried in the unkind soil.

At last, on 16 April, they reached Gondokoro. Nobody had been told that Gordon was coming: nobody knew who he was. The troops of the Egyptian garrison were receiving supplies of gin and slave girls instead of payment; their morale was appalling, and none of them dared move more than half a mile from the camp for fear of being attacked by natives. The town itself was little more than a clearing in the forest: a sparse collection of mud huts, swaddled in hot moisture and rotten with insects and disease. This was the capital of Gordon's empire; the seat of his government; the hub of a world that he had to restore to life. The awfulness of it all made him wonder. At first, the plump figure of the Khedive had amused him. Now, the ruler worried him. Why had he really engaged him? Was he sincere about cutting out the slave trade – root, crop and proverbial branch? Or had he been appointed as a kind of figurehead: somebody who would catch the attention of the British people, assist Khedive Ismail in his dealings with the creditors, and make everything seem to be a great deal better than it really was?

That first night at Gondokoro, Gordon must have been more than usually grateful that his supreme commander was God. With any more fallible power, the prospect would have been terrible beyond description. As things were, Gordon's spirit

– which seemed to function with the same tripping energy as his body – perked up. By the following day, he had issued his first declaration: ivory was declared a Sudanese government monopoly, and no further imports of arms or ammunition would be permitted. He had also worked out his plan for dealing with the slave trade.

As all Gordon's plans, it went right to the heart of the matter. If the slave trade was to be abolished, the dealers would have to be cut off from their source of supply – and, indeed, from their markets. This could most simply done by building a line of fortified posts along the banks of the White Nile – from its junction with the Sobat River, a few hundred miles to the north of Gondokoro, to as far as they could penetrate to the south. Armed river steamers would patrol this length of the waterway; and, while they were establishing the posts, they could explore the route to the great lakes.

But this was only part of the problem. In setting up and maintaining this system of policing, Gordon would be compelled to delegate responsibility to officers of doubtful integrity. They would have to be set an example. 'The main point,' he wrote, 'is to be just and straightforward, to fear no one or no one's saying, to avoid all tergiversation or twisting, even if you lose by it, and to be *hard to all* if they do not obey you.' Somehow, he would also have to win the trust of the natives. Many of them were terrorized by the threat of slavery, and afraid to grow anything in the way of an adequate crop for fear that somebody would move in, burn the huts down, and take the harvest away. Gordon was by no means daunted by this aspect of the assignment: he determined to give the natives the one thing they had never had – a square deal. He would buy their ivory from them at a fair price, either for cash or cows. He would protect them against the slavers and the pillagers, he would do whatever a man could do under the circumstances to bring them security.

He decided to build his first fort at the junction of the White Nile and the Sobat, but nothing could be done before the stores arrived. Stores which were left to their own devices in the Sudan had a habit of never arriving at all. After six days at Gondokoro, Gordon decided to go back to Khartoum to hurry them up. He also had one or two points that he wished to discuss with the governor-general.

He made the trip north in eleven days. Ismail Ayoub Pasha was delighted to see his distinguished colleague, and he ushered him into the relative cool of the palace. Gordon wasted no time on preliminary skirmishing: he went straight into the assault. After he had been speaking for a few minutes, the smile on Ayoub's face had frozen. By the time he had finished, it had vanished completely.

Did the governor-general realize that the Egyptian government had no effective authority anywhere to the south of Khartoum: that its fortunes were entirely in the hands of troops who were demoralized and seldom paid, and officials who were rotten with corruption? If Gordon was going to run Equatoria, he was determined to pay his way. The only way in which he could measure his success was to insist that his financial accounts should be kept apart from those of the Sudan itself. This, he shrewdly estimated, would lessen Ayoub's authority over him – and stop his using the Equatorial provinces as a screen for his own economic inadequacy.

Raouf Pasha, the young Egyptian who had been attached to his staff had already shown himself to be useless and, which was even worse, dishonest. He must go. Finally, Gordon insisted the troops should be paid properly. If Ayoub Pasha didn't like his demands, he could appeal to Cairo, but it was not hard to guess what the answer would be. The Khedive had virtually given Gordon *carte blanche*: he did not mind what action he took so long as he produced results. As the following year was to show, Gordon was right in keeping his accounts to himself. From being a constant drain on the Egyptian exchequer, the Equatorial province suddenly became profitable. The Khedive received £48,000 and a further £60,000 were salted away in a reserve fund.

The meeting with Ayoub Pasha had been acrimonious, but Gordon was too busy to worry about that. His stores were now

116

waiting at Berber. Acting on the principle that (as he put it) 'self is the best staff officer', he hurried downstream to get them moving. Later, he was to observe that 'the best servant I ever had was myself! I always do what I like.' Both statements help to sum up Gordon's role in Equatoria. Although, by title, the province's governor-general, he filled, at one time or another, the roles of soldier, sick-bay attendant, accountant, dealer, storekeeper, welfare officer, transport manager, merchant, and cook. Throughout the period, he seemed to be driven by an almost supernatural energy. It would have been impressive enough in a temperate climate: in a country so close to the Equator, it was almost beyond belief.

Within a surprisingly short space of time, he was back at Gondokoro with the stores, and preparing for the trip to the junction with the Sobat river. Two forts were to be built: one at the junction, and one, roughly midway from Gondokoro, at Shambé. He would take charge of operations at the former: Gessi and his nephew, Anson Gordon, would look after things at Shambé. Gordon had not been at the northern post for long, when he struck his first blow against the slave trade. A letter was intercepted from a dealer to the Egyptian commander at Fashoda. The officer was told to expect a caravan of sixteen hundred slaves and two thousand head of stolen cattle. Payment for safe conduct would be at the usual rate of £70 (sic) per slave. The message gave details of the route – and even with his inadequate force of Arab soldiers, Gordon had no difficulty in intercepting the convoy. The slaves were set free; the cattle were returned to their owners; and the slave handler's troops were ordered to go back to their homes (most of them near Khartoum). Those of his own men who turned out to be troublesome were also sent back to Khartoum.

Gordon spent eight weeks at Sobat. The heat was terrible, and sickness was already beginning to affect the European members of his staff. He, himself, was fit – though given to spasms of irritability. Nevertheless, he had no doubts about the success of his labours. 'To do anything,' he wrote to Augusta, 'there is nothing like beginning on a small scale, and

117

directing your energy like a squirt, at one particular thing.'
In another letter, he said: 'I apprehend not the least difficulty
in the work; the greatest will be to gain the people's confidence again. They have been badly treated.'

On the way back to Gondokoro, he stopped at Shambé to
pick up Gessi and Anson Gordon. Things were in a terrible
state. Anson had already died of fever, and the Italian was
seriously ill. By September, Linant was dead, most of the
others were ill, and Gordon had to apply for two officers from
the Royal Engineers to augment his dwindling establishment.
He himself remained well – a condition he attributed to faith.
'Fellows think they have it [fever],' he observed, 'and they do.
I didn't think so, and I didn't get it. Fear of death brings
death.' On a more down-to-earth basis, he instructed his
subordinates never to 'forget their mosquito curtains'; con-
sume plenty of quinine; and to take regular doses of what he
described as 'a splendid daily pill'. The prescription was $\frac{1}{2}$ gr.
of ginger, $\frac{1}{2}$ gr. of ipecacuanha and 3 grs. of rhubarb. Gordon,
like most Victorians, believed in keeping the bowels open.
Later on, he put much of his pharmaceutical faith in Dover's
powders – a remedy which combined ipecacuanha and opium.
It might, conceivably, have been the reason for Mrs Asquith's
belief that he was an opium eater.

He had no misgivings about his ability as an *ex tempore*
medico. In one letter, he referred to himself proudly as 'one
of the best doctors . . . that I know'. Nevertheless, paddling
about in wet tents, which had become saturated by the heavy
rain, ministering to his sick officers, *and* trying to get on with
the business of governing Equatoria imposed a severe strain on
him. He had been compelled to give up his tent to one of the
Englishmen who, if he pulled through, would have to be sent
home. When he did get an opportunity to lie down, he was
kept awake by rats fighting on the top of his mosquito net.
He constructed a rat trap from a pencil, a piece of tin, and
an old dispatch case, and it was effective up to a point.

Gordon became more and more irritable. He was well, he
assured Augusta, 'but a shadow'. 'Add to this [the sickness] all

the intrigues about me, a large amount of works of all sorts and preparations to make. Letters of all sorts, the accounts of the dead now all finished and you will see your brother is bothered.'

His standby throughout this period should have been his chief of staff – an American named Chaillé-Long, who held the rank of colonel with the Egyptian army. He was a small man, with a large nose and an equally big moustache, who had already shown himself to be a great deal less competent than Gordon's first impressions had suggested. Even before they reached Gondokoro, Gordon was writing: 'The American is a regular failure. He is so feeble, he can do nothing at all. He lives on what he *has* done, and of course that does not help what has *to be* done now. His object is to prove to me that he is not to blame: another useless thing, for it is not a judgement I have to pronounce . . .' The best thing to do with Chaillé-Long was to get rid of him. He was sent down to Uganda escorted by two soldiers with instructions to begin negotiations for a treaty with King M'Tesa. Possibly the monarch would succumb to his words which, on the whole, were more effective than his actions.

In spite of the sickness of his staff, Gordon was beginning to make an impression on the province. He taught the natives how to husband their crops, and how to use money. Those in distress were treated to a glimpse of the Gordon who had done so much for the poor of Gravesend. One of his soldiers had a child wife of only twelve years old. The man beat her, and, one night, she came to the fire where Gordon was sitting. She was shivering. Gordon sent for an interpreter to find out what she wanted. She explained what was happening, and he sent her on board his steamer. She was given the choice of returning to her husband or going free. 'The girl would not go back,' Gordon wrote, 'so she stays on the steamer.'

A woman whom he described as 'a poor old bag of bones', was discovered starving to death. She was brought into the camp and food was prepared for her. But it was too late. She 'died very quietly', he had to report. On another occasion,

119

Gordon was awakened in the middle of a dismally wet night by a child crying. He went out of his tent and saw that a girl was lying in a large puddle of water apparently dead. Nobody paid any attention to her. He ordered her to be buried, and then he noticed, in the long grass nearby, a baby of about one year old. He picked the child up and carried her to his tent. On the way, he noticed that the girl had not yet been buried. He was about to hurry the men up, when he realized that she was still alive. She was taken into a hut, made comfortable in front of a fire, and given brandy. On the following morning, she was still alive and the child was gulping down milk. The young woman died later, but the infant was, as Gordon put it, 'in for the pilgrimage of life'.

Incidents such as these were talked about. They established Gordon as a just and kindly ruler, and the people began to love him. Before very long, he was able to take walks far away from the camp without the slightest danger. An Egyptian official, on the other hand, would have needed a regiment to give him safe escort. At about this time, the military problem was solved. The Egyptian troops were bad soldiers: they found the climate hard to endure and they were lazy. The local enemy was a tribe named the Baris, who had little more than spears in their armoury, but they were more than a match for the listless men. Consequently, Gordon decided to create his own force. The recruits came from a tribe of cannibals named the Niam Niam. To begin with, he enlisted fifty of them: they were excellent fighters, armed with rifles and spears. By the end of 1876, he had five hundred of them – thickset, sturdy men who had all the qualities the Egyptians so lamentably lacked.

On 18 October, Chaillé-Long returned from Uganda. His conversations with King M'Tesa had been fruitless, and he told a harrowing story of how he and his two men had been forced to fight their way back. It would have made an excellent article for *Blackwood's Magazine*, but Gordon knew his Chaillé-Long well enough to discount much of it. Nevertheless, the man was clearly exhausted, and he departed for a rest in Khartoum. He said that he would be away for six weeks. A week later, the engineer, Kemp, went down with fever. He was the only member of the original team of Europeans who was still at Gondokoro. As Gordon told Augusta:

I have been so cross since I wrote to you – and why? The reason is that I was made ill by the utter feebleness of my staff. My friend Kemp came back sick; took possession of me as a servant, and of my things as his; lost his own bed; took mine. I got wet, and a chill; and it was only by a severe course of pills that I am all right again. I have now given orders that all illness is to take place away from me; and the staff are not to come near me except on duty.

Fortunately Kemp recovered and was able to resume his duties. Meanwhile, two young officers from the Royal Engineers, Lieutenant Watson and Lieutenant Chippindall, were on their way south – accompanied by Ernest Linant, the deceased French interpreter's brother.

Gordon had asked for the two sapper officers specifically. They were young ('no man over forty should come here, and then only those who are accustomed to these climates') and they had been well spoken of. Watson's admiration for his new commander was immediate and absolute. 'I do not wonder at people liking Chinese Gordon,' he wrote in a letter home. 'You would if you knew him, I am sure.' Chippindall was less certain. 'He seems to think that nobody but his blessed self can even screw a box lid on,' he remarked. 'He is a fearful egotist in that way.' 'But,' he added, 'he is devilish kind to one, and really I fear he will almost spoil me for future service.' Later on, the admiration was to be rather one-sided. 'These two,' Gordon wrote, 'Watson and Chipp have cost nearly £3,000 between them and done nothing.'

But this was from a Gordon who had decided that 'there is now not one thing I value in the world. Its honours – they are false. Its knick-knacks – they are perishable and useless. Whilst I live, I value God's blessing – health; and if you have that, as far as the world goes, you are rich.'

When Chippindall referred to Gordon's pride in the matter of screwing on box lids, he was, perhaps, being unkind. Gordon was, as it happened, extremely good with his hands. Once, when he had nothing better to do, he built a rocket gun out of a length of pipe which had been thrown away. He used to enjoy repairing watches and clocks; sometimes he would take a watch to pieces and reassemble it – just for fun. Indeed, his main contribution to diplomatic relations with the King of Uganda was to repair a musical box that the sovereign had entrusted to his skill.

Abou Said, who should have been Gordon's trusted lieutenant, had proved himself to be no better than his past had indicated. He began to treat his commanding officer with insubordination and even tried to take over some of his functions. This was irritating enough: what was worse, however, was the fact that he was helping himself from the government store of ivory – and, at the same time, trying to stir up a mutiny. Gordon summed up his past, present, and probable future character in a few well-selected words. When the storm at last died down, Abou Said found himself on his way back to Cairo in a native boat. There, the authorities could be relied on to return him to the prison whence he had come.

In the summer of 1875, there were reports of trouble at Sobat. Gordon hurried off downstream in the steamer to investigate what turned out to be a false alarm. To his surprise (and, it must be admitted, to his indignation), he found that one of the Englishmen who had been invalided home was there. He had made a complete recovery, which might have been seen as an occasion for pleasure. Gordon, however, concluded that he had grossly exaggerated his symptoms, and had been shipped off unnecessarily. A man was required to keep going until he dropped. This officer had committed the unforgivable sin of *pretending* to drop. The governor-general made it quite clear that he had no further use for him.

Meanwhile Chaillé-Long's six-week period of leave had extended itself to twelve weeks, and he had taken the opportunity to visit Cairo. The message announcing his impending return also reported that he was bringing 150 reinforcements. Of the Egyptians stationed at Gondokoro, half of the 250 men who had come south with Gordon had died within six months of arrival, and 100 of them had been invalided home. At one time, he had only 25 soldiers fit for duty. By now, Gordon had moved his headquarters a few miles downstream to Lado – a village which, in his unquenchable optimism, he had decided possessed a more salubrious climate. Even so, he did not want any more Egyptian soldiers. Perhaps Chaillé-Long had been sensible enough to bring native troops. For a few days, he was kept in suspense. Then, the chief of staff and his men arrived. They were all Egyptians. By the following day, 84 were already on the sick list – and this was a time of year which was reputed to be 'the Healthy Season'. If Chaillé-Long expected a hero's welcome, he was to be disappointed.

Chaillé-Long and Gordon were temperamentally incompatible: there was no doubt about that. Gordon was sincere, direct, a man of action. Chaillé-Long, on the other hand, was a very indifferent soldier with a talent for public relations. The first meeting with him was impressive. On closer acquaintance, however, he turned out to be vague, neglectful and procrastinating. 'I took the opportunity,' Gordon wrote, 'when we were in good tempers, to point out to him that we should never be able to get on with one another when near one another.' After a succession of rows, the only thing for it seemed to be that they should split up. The break came at the American's suggestion. He reminded Gordon of an idea of his to land an expedition at Mombasa: march the four hundred miles on to Uganda over the more healthy, hilly, country – and establish a trading link between Lake Victoria and the Red Sea. Suppose he went back to Cairo and gave the Khedive an outline of the scheme? Gordon agreed with, perhaps, rather too much alacrity. At all events, Chaillé-Long bore a grudge which, later on, was to mar the Gordon legend.

When he reached Cairo somewhat the worse in health he was warmly received by the Khedive – who sent him off to the south of France on sick leave. On his return, he was told that the overland expedition from the Red Sea had been approved, and that he should lead it. His instructions were in the form of sealed orders, which were not to be opened until he was travelling down the Suez Canal.

For some inexplicable reason, the Khedive had accepted the spirit of the plan rather than the letter of it. Instead of setting off from Mombasa, as Gordon had suggested, they were to take a different route, using Kismayu as the point of departure. When he heard about it, the Sultan of Zanzibar became disturbed at Egyptian activity so close to his frontier, and cabled his objections to Lord Derby, the English foreign minister. The British government was sympathetic: Derby, in his turn, protested to the Khedive and, on Christmas Day 1875, Chaillé-Long was instructed to return to Cairo. At this point, he might have vanished from the pages of history – had it not been for a book entitled *My Life In Four Continents*, which he published in 1912.

If Mrs Asquith had the impression that Gordon was an opium eater because he was a firm believer in that popular specific, Dover's powders, his undeserved reputation as an alcoholic came from Chaillé-Long's writing. *My Life In Four Continents*, was a very average book, and unlikely to endure. Unfortunately, however, it was one of the sources used by a far more gifted writer, Lytton Strachey, when he set about compiling his portrait of Gordon for Eminent Victorians.

In his fits of melancholy [Strachey wrote] he would shut himself in his tent for days at a time, with a hatchet and a flag placed at the door to indicate that he was not to be disturbed for any reason whatever; until at last the cloud would lift, the signals would be removed, and the Governor would appear brisk and cheerful. During one of these retirements, there was a grave danger of a native attack upon the camp. Colonel Chaillé-Long, the Chief of Staff, ventured after some hesitation, to ignore the flag and hatchet, and to enter the forbidden tent. He found Gordon seated at a table, upon which were an open Bible and an open bottle of brandy (compare this with Chaillé-Long's description of their first encounter in Cairo; the open Bible and the open bottle). Long explained the circumstances, but could obtain no answer beyond the abrupt words – 'You are commander of the camp' – and was obliged to retire, nonplussed, to deal with the situation as best he could. On the following morning, Gordon, cleanly shaven, and in the full-dress uniform of the Royal Engineers, entered Long's hut with his usual tripping step, exclaiming – 'Old fellow, now don't be angry with me. I was very low last night. Let's have a good breakfast – a little b. and s. Do you feel up to it?'

On such was Gordon's reputation as an alcoholic based. During those days of solitude, he was, by implication, demolishing the camp's supplies of brandy: drowning, as they say, his sorrows – and there must have been plenty of them to drown, each magnified by the depressive effects of the climate. Gordon drank brandy – obviously. It was at once the social drink of gentlemen of his time, and the universally accepted remedy for tropical maladies. It was obvious that he would have a bottle in his tent, and that he took doses of it along with his quinine, his rhubarb pills, and his Dover's powders. It is also likely that there were times when he was not to be disturbed. For want of an efficient staff, he was all things to all men at his headquarters. People would trouble him with trifling matters, which could easily have been dealt with by somebody else. If he were to commune with God, and write his long letters to Augusta, and relax in any way at all, he needed to have some time to himself.

It is quite likely that Chaillé-Long did burst in on his privacy one day. The American *was* supposed to be in charge of the troops, and Gordon may well have been testy. There are, however, no reports of native attacks on the camp: this, like the implied brandy jags and the somewhat stilted dialogue about not being angry, 'Old fellow', and 'how about a b. and

s.?' sound like the products of Chaillé-Long's invention. For
Strachey, in his mission to prove that all Victorians were not
eminent, it provided useful ammunition. If Gordon did have a
weakness, it was more likely that he was a hypochondriac. He
was forever dosing himself and worrying about his suspected
angina (which, incidentally, he never had). The state of his
liver also concerned him: he believed that brandy was bad for
it, and on a number of occasions, gave up drinking it completely.

Gordon did not subdue the people of Equatoria: he encouraged them. They never regarded him as a tyrant – after their
fashion, they loved him. By 1875, there was almost a tranquillity and certainly a ripening prosperity in the land. It remained, however, to make the expedition to the great lakes.
Gordon was not anxious to go on it. He mistrusted geographers
and believed that they were given too much acclaim. He
talked scathingly about 'the inordinate praise which is given
to an explorer'. He also disliked the idea of the trip; the
thought of 'being boxed up for a phantasy in a 50-ft long
steamer for a fortnight'. It would, he said, 'be my death'. It
obviously would have been nothing of the kind: he had been
'boxed up' for much longer periods before now, and he had
never wilted.

At times, he seems to have entertained the dream of a
Central African empire. At others, he was a prey to disenchantment. He hated the unctuous officials who agreed, and
smiled, and did nothing. He was repelled by the thought that
Egyptians from Gondokoro to Cairo were up to their necks
in the slave trade, and regarded its suppression as a piece of
pious propaganda. Each day, in his imagination, he wrote his
resignation to the Khedive – and, each day, he decided to
soldier on.

He may not have been anxious to become an explorer, but
at least one member of that illustrious profession counted himself among Gordon's admirers. Sir Richard Burton's description of his first meeting was a beautiful example of those

somewhat purple snatches which people were apt to write about Gordon.

I was astonished to find how unlike were all his portraits [he wrote]. No photograph has represented those calm, benevolent blue eyes and that modest, reserved and even shy expression, blent with simple dignity, which, where he was intimate, changed to the sympathetic frankness of a child's face.

Gordon was equally, though less rapturously, taken with the explorer. Later on, he was to offer him an important job. Burton, it seemed, was content to keep his devotion within the bounds of reason – at any rate, he turned it down.

But, like it or not, Gordon had to make the journey to the lakes. It was not, simply, a question of going there and coming back. Posts had to be built at frequent intervals on the banks of the river. The idea was that, in the event of an attack by the natives, a traveller could hurry to one or another of them for safety. There were also maps to be made, and there was certainly no better cartographer than Gordon. He would have to run the risk of being praised: his professional services were needed. Eventually, he began to share the general fascination with the inland seas, which had been merely glimpsed by white men, and which now seemed to hold so much promise. After one angry letter to the Khedive, he suspected that he might be relieved of his appointment – and acknowledged 'to feeling a sort of regret if I have to leave before opening the river to the lakes.' 'But,' he added quickly, 'it would soon pass.' At about this time, possibly as the result of comments from Augusta, he showed an uncharacteristic concern for the punctuation of his letters – which was always original, and sometimes non-existent. 'Are my stops better?' he asked, 'I never learnt grammar nor dancing.' It was typical of his changing moods: the zoom lens of his mind, which travelled from the large and the general to the small and particular with such speed.

Originally, he had intended to send two columns south. One,

headed by Chippindall, was to make for Lake Albert: the other, with Linant in charge, would blaze the trail to Lake Victoria. In Equatorial Africa, however, it was unwise to make any plan involving people too long before the event: one never knew who would be available. Chippindall, like so many of the Europeans, fell sick, and had to be sent home. Fortunately, the faithful and indestructible Romolo Gessi was present, and Gordon decided that he should take charge of the whole expedition. Then, almost at the last moment, he changed his mind. No doubt after long consultations, with the Almighty, he decided to come too. The decision followed 'something like a stroke of paralysis', which he attributed to too much smoking. He resolved to cut it down.

By the summer of 1875, they were on their way. It was very rough going indeed: the river banks overgrown with thick vegetation and the climate worse than ever. From the hinterland, there were often ominous noises, which suggested that the natives were not necessarily friendly. On one occasion, when the steamer was in difficulties, a party of warriors, who lived in a village overlooking the river, attacked them. They were beaten off, but Gordon had misgivings about the following day – when they would all be busy with the ship. Ernest Linant was given a party of forty troops and told to burn their huts down. At least it might act as a distraction. During the morning, Linant encountered no opposition. In the afternoon, however, his small force was ambushed. Only four men survived. Among the casualties was the young Frenchman.

Gordon was sympathetic to the coloured people. 'The natives are brave fellows,' he wrote, 'they know that our soldiers cannot hit them in most cases when they fire, and so in they rush and it is over.' And: 'We derided these poor blacks who fought for their independence ... I declare, in spite of the expressions you may note in my letters, I truly sympathize with them. They say, "We do not want your cloth and beads; you go your way, and we will go ours. We do not want to see your chief." '

The last major obstacle before Lake Albert was a cataract,

three miles long, which disrupted the Nile at Dufilé. The steamer had to be taken to pieces, manhandled overland, and then reassembled. Gessi, with Kemp providing technical skills, took charge of the operation. All that Gordon could do was wait. It was a difficult, nerve-stretching period, and hardly the time to receive a querulous letter from the Khedive. When he had read it, Gordon became angry. He drafted three telegrams of resignation, and prepared to return north. On the following morning, however, some more mail arrived. It should have come earlier by special messenger, but the unfortunate man had been killed somewhere along the route. This correspondence was in a very different vein. On a sad note, the Khedive explained about the expedition down the Red Sea, and its failure to get beyond the coast. On a more pleasant key, he was full of praise for Gordon and all his works. The telegrams of resignation were cancelled. 'The man had gone to all this expense under the belief that I would stick by him; I could not therefore leave him,' Gordon explained afterwards.

Doubtless his mood of the previous evening had been occasioned by his surroundings. It was, he said, in one of his weekly letters to Augusta, 'a dead mournful spot, with a heavy damp penetrating everything ... you have little idea of the silence and solitude. I am sure no one whom God did not support could bear up. It is simply killing.'

By 29 April 1876, the work was done. Gessi had circumnavigated Lake Albert in the steamer with its little ten horse power engine, which had stood up to so much misuse from the harsh river. He reported that it was smaller than he had thought – about fifty miles across: that violent storms swept over it, and that there were numerous, and unfriendly, natives on either bank. There were no cries of welcome; but, rather, angry shouts of: 'Go on! Go on! We want no Turks here.'

To reach Lake Victoria entailed travelling through Uganda, and there were difficulties. Although King M'Tesa declared himself to be a Christian, he had a healthy mistrust of Turks, Arabs, and white men. Perhaps he had taken note of the words spoken by his colleague-in-monarchy, the King of Zululand. As the latter very neatly put it: 'First come missionary, then trader, then soldier – when soldier comes, it is all over with black man.' At any rate, M'Tesa was not going to allow any trade routes for Egypt to pass through his land. A garrison of one hundred and sixty Sudanese troops, under an Arab officer, had been stationed in the royal capital at M'Tesa's request. Now, the men were suddenly held prisoner. Gordon's first instinct was to march in and rescue them by force. In the end, however, prudence prevailed. After a series of forced marches, in which he covered fifteen miles a day through this impossible territory, he reached a small village on the Nile. From there, through a German employed as medical officer to Equatoria, and who happened to be visiting M'Tesa's court, he persuaded the unpredictable sovereign to release the men. In return, Gordon promised to recognize Uganda's independence.

There were a few more surveys to be carried out, and then his work was done. In November, he passed north through Khartoum with, so the story goes, a black boy and a lion cub. At the beginning of December he was in Cairo, telling the Khedive that he was intending to resign. The Khedive said neither 'yes' nor 'no'. He urged him to go back to England for a rest, and wished him a happy Christmas. On Christmas Eve, Gordon arrived in London. Four days later, *The Times* printed a long appreciation of his work in Equatoria. In an admirably balanced account, the writer (Captain Burnaby, no doubt) pointed out that 'Colonel Gordon acted as merchant as well as explorer and ruler, and traded with great success' – something which would be 'particularly appreciated by our anxious English creditors'. Gordon may have been grateful for this appreciation of his business acumen. During his next chapter of service, he was to find himself in a jungle far more dangerous than that of Equatoria, and where the natives were less friendly than the tribes of mid-Africa. In this case, however, the jungle was Cairo and the unfriendly warriors were European businessmen.

8
The Outstanding Problems

Gordon was not a man who put much value in good food and comfort. Nevertheless, before he left Equatoria, he had said that he was looking forward to the luxuries of England. The three prospects which appealed to him particularly were travelling first class on trains; lying in bed until 11 a.m.; and eating oysters ('not a dozen, but four dozen', he said. They were, he observed, 'good for the brain'). He arrived in London at 7 p.m. on Christmas Eve 1876, and installed himself in rooms in Cecil Street, just off the Strand. He was feeling, as he told Mrs Freese when he went to see her, 'tired, tired and no earthly rest will give me quiet'. He had intended to spend six months recuperating, but the introduction to this period of leisure did not live up to his expectations. His leave was, he said in a mood of self-pity, 'one continual misery'.

Why? There was plenty to occupy it: visits to Augusta down at Southampton, to brothers Henry and Enderby at Woolwich, and to the always faithful Freeses. Officially, he had to make calls at the War Office and Foreign Office, and there was an almost continuous traffic of telegrams and letters to and from Cairo. He could not complain of not having enough to do. Was his conscience bothering him? As *The Times* pointed out, he had accomplished the greater part of his assignment 'so quietly that it has been somewhat undervalued'. The road was open from Cairo to Lake Albert. The natives were now ready to 'barter ivory for beads, cows, powder, and other goods'. It had been an almost overwhelmingly difficult task, 'yet he latterly ruled his Province with ease, and has left order and tranquillity behind him.' As the newspaper happily reported, the improvements were such, that, even when he was deep in the jungle, he was able to receive his copies of *The Times* a mere seven weeks after their publication in London. All this was, surely enough. Nobody could have accomplished more. By all that was reasonable, he was entitled to give up his African assignment.

And yet, as he must have been uncomfortably aware, there was one job which was still not completed. He had harassed the slave trade: certainly. But this was all. Zebehr was in sullen exile in Cairo; but his son, Suleiman, had taken over his role of uncrowned monarch of Darfur. The Egyptian garrisons to the north of Equatoria were as limp and ineffectual as ever; the officials were still augmenting their incomes with handsome rewards for looking away when slave convoys went through. The fact of the matter, as Gordon knew only too well, was that nobody, really, wished to see the slave trade abolished. It dated back almost to the beginnings of history: it was one of the traditional industries of the Moslem world. And, as the people in Khartoum might have pointed out, what else did they have to export? Nothing grew in the desert: nothing was manufactured. Humanity was the only merchandise they had to offer.

It was all very well for anti-slavery organizations in England to raise their voices in protest: reality was a long distance away, and the essence of it was an army of officials who depended on this pernicious commerce for their incomes. Gordon himself had made frequent protests to the Khedive about the quality of his administration, and the Khedive had agreed with him. At their last meeting in Cairo, he had assured Gordon that he was as anxious as ever to put an end to this traffic in humanity. Corruption, he had promised, would be ruthlessly punished. The army and the civil service would be purged until they were both splendid examples of integrity.

Did Gordon believe him? Probably not. Khedive Ismail was, he suspected, no better than the rest – despite all his pious talk. His paramount problem was the state of his country's finances, which became worse with every day that passed. He was a profligate spender, determined to enjoy all the status symbols of his period. There had to be railways and steamers (nowadays, emergent states find a similar satisfaction in creating airlines), and he was determined that his personal prestige should be reflected in his palaces. His troops and minor functionaries seldom received regular wages, but this did not stop him from spending £11 million on one residential showpiece. This state of affairs could continue only for as long as his European creditors were prepared to renew their loans. If proposals to abolish slavery produced a good impression overseas, he would certainly support them.

When he had left Cairo, Gordon was under the impression that his resignation had been accepted. The Khedive, on the other hand, was equally certain that his dissatisfaction was nothing more than could be cured by a rest in Europe. After an exchange of telegrams, Gordon agreed to return on condition that he was appointed governor-general of the entire Sudan. Somewhat to his surprise, the Khedive agreed. 'I have,' the ruler's final shot in this exchange of messages read, 'decided to unite, under one general government, all Sudan, Darfur, and the Equatorial provinces, and to confide to you the important mission of directing it.' Three governors would be appointed to serve under him: one for the Sudan and Equatoria, one for Darfur, and the third for the Red Sea coast and the eastern Sudan. The appointment was, Ismail stressed, completely independent of the Egyptian ministry of finances – in other words, he would be responsible to the sovereign and nobody else. 'I end,' the telegram concluded, 'in thanking you, my dear Gordon, for your goodness and for continuing to give Egypt your precious services, and I am convinced that, with your great experience and your devotion, we shall bring to a magnificent conclusion the work that we are carrying out.' On the day following the receipt of this message, Gordon set off for Africa. Two months after his return to London, he was back in Khartoum. He was now in charge of over a million square miles of territory. As proof of his friendship, the Khedive had made him a field marshal in

the Egyptian army (he was still only a lieutenant-colonel in
the Royal Engineers), and had presented him with a uniform
decorated with a hundred and fifty pounds worth of gold
lace. He had also conferred upon him the Grand Cordon of
the Medjidieh Order. Finally, as if Gordon had not already
enough to keep him busy, he had vested in him the further
responsibility of acting as envoy extraordinary to Abyssinia.

Diplomatic relations between Egypt and Abyssinia were
habitually strained to breaking point: and, frequently, they
broke. Although the latter country was extremely primitive,
and its ruler – a self-proclaimed Christian of dubious sanity
named King Johannis – incapable of making any decision
that seemed to be based on reason, the Abyssinians were much
better fighters than the Egyptians. Chaillé-Long, in a series of
engagements in which false heroics were only matched by
appalling mismanagement, had once succeeded in losing 10,000
Egyptian troops, 25 cannons and 10,000 Remington rifles.
This sort of thing, obviously, could not be allowed to continue. If King Johannis could not be thrashed as Sir Robert
Napier had chastized his father, the only solution was to seek
some sort of friendship. Perhaps, the Khedive suggested,
Gordon would like to see what could be done on his way back
to the Sudan?

For the time being, as Gordon quickly discovered, nothing
could be done. The king was away, fighting a war somewhere.
Gordon left a letter for him, and then hurried westwards to
Khartoum, covering thirty miles a day on his camel. During
the coming twelve months, he was to cover four thousand
miles by this method. It was just as well that he enjoyed it.

He was elated, but 'only slightly', by the honours that the
Khedive had conferred upon him, and he used to refer to
his field marshal's uniform as his 'golden armour'. He intended
to wear it in situations where, for want of anything else, his
only weapon would be prestige. These would be frequent, and
he realized it.

I have to contend [he wrote] with many vested interests,

with fanaticism ... with wild independent tribes of Bedouins, with inefficient governors, and with a large semi-independent province lately under Zebehr Pasha at Bahr el Gazal. ... With terrific exertion, in two or three years' time I may, with God's administration, make a good province, with a good army, and a fair revenue and peace, and also have suppressed the slave trade.*

There were many Gordons: Soldier Gordon, Saint Gordon, Tourist Gordon, and Optimist Gordon. There were times when his mood sank to utter despondency, and he wanted to be done with his work – even, with life itself. But, in moments of challenge, Optimist Gordon always prevailed, even when everything suggested that the situation was hopeless. For much of his career, it was his strength: in the final analysis, however, it became his weakness.

He arrived at Khartoum on 3 May 1877. If his predecessor, Ismail Ayoub Pasha, had not taken kindly to his dismissal, the former governor-general's sister had been even more displeased. She had broken most of the windows in the palace, and had shredded the cushions on the divan into worthless scraps of silk. However, the staff seemed to be intact, and he noted that his personal servants included a eunuch to look after his harem. In view of his attitude to women, the job was now something of a sinecure.

In spite of the blazing heat, he got down to work at once. Within fifteen days, he had composed his first proclamation, which was read aloud by the mayor of Khartoum in the public square. Gordon stood by and watched, and presently mumbled something about 'With the help of God, I will hold the balance level.' Everybody politely applauded.

The proclamation was an impressive document. It abolished the use of the raw hide whip, which was the time-honoured method of getting better results from slaves and servants. A box for petitions was to be installed at the palace gate. The corruption of clerks was to be checked; and a project for

* *The Times*, more realistically, assessed the time required as fifty years.

pumping water from the river to the town was to be investi-
gated. The Turkish second-in-command was sacked on the
spot: Gordon's own clerk was to follow him into the wilderness. In spite of the third point in the proclamation, he continued to accept bribes discreetly. By the time he was found
out, this very minor official had salted away £3,000.

Having issued his first statement of policy, Gordon got down
to the much more difficult part of the assignment – that of
abolishing the slave trade. Back in England, the Anti-Slavery
Society urged with the pragmatism that is the luxury of those
who are thousands of miles away, that he should employ
drastic methods. When his policy became clear, its members
criticized him for not being radical enough. They also deplored
a not unreasonable action of his – in which he himself bought
slaves and then enlisted them into his forces. Gordon who, it
had to be admitted, could take a much more realistic view of
the situation, came to the conclusion that there was a limit to
what he could achieve immediately. It might be a humane and
inspiring idea to demand that everybody at present in captivity should be granted his or her freedom, but it was mani-
festly impossible. The system was far too deeply embedded in
the Moslem culture. Nor had he anything like sufficient troops
to enforce such a regulation. The best he could hope to do was
to introduce controls.

The document he eventually produced had four main points
to it. He demanded that all slaves should be registered by
1 January of the following year. On the other hand, runaway
slaves (and this was one of the items that the Anti-Slavery
Society objected to) were to be returned to their owners –
unless there was any evidence to show that they had been
cruelly treated. If they had not been registered, they would not
be sent back. Finally, no slaves could be registered after New
Year's Day, 1878 – which was another way of saying that
nobody could be pressed into slavery after that date.

If the people in London thought that he was being too
moderate, he would have explained that he could not expect
the slaves to trust him, if they saw that he was (or seemed to

be) unjust to their owners. He might have added the suggestion that the Anti-Slavery Society's views were not subjected to the pressures which affected his own attitude. He did not expect even these measures to be popular. Indeed, when describing them to Augusta, he asked: 'Who that had not the Almighty with him would dare to do that? I will do it; for I value my life as naught.' Certainly, the resolutions of the Anglo-Egyptian convention on the slave trade, which was held later that year, were much more insipid. The sale of slaves from one family to another was prohibited, but this was not to come into force until a period of seven years had elapsed in Cairo, twelve years in the Sudan. After that, anyone convicted of the offence was liable to a term of anything from five months to five years imprisonment. A person who was caught dealing in slaves was to be considered guilty of stealing with murder. The British view was that it should be punished by death. The Egyptian opinion was, as nearly always, ambiguous. Gordon decided that, since his terms of reference made him virtual dictator of the Sudan and its subject states, he would use his own discretion.

Two weeks after arriving in Khartoum, he set out for Darfur. The reason for Khedive Pasha's anxiety for his recall was already uncomfortably clear: Darfur was in a state of revolt. Sixteen thousand Egyptian troops were cut off at El Fasher. Zebehr's son, Suleiman, had taken over the south of the country. A scarcely less villainous character named Haroun was in control of the north. Gordon decided to reduce Haroun to subjection first, and then turn his forces on to Suleiman. The question was: what forces? He had about five hundred men available at Khartoum. In Darfur, the garrisons were, to say the least, unreliable.

Darfur was a large expanse of desert. The frontier was four hundred miles to the west of Khartoum: beyond that the centres of population were grouped around the water wells, which were anything from thirty to sixty miles apart. The morale of the Egyptian garrisons was appalling. One outpost had received no pay for three years: another had been without any news for one and a half years. Without money to spend, the men's only source of subsistence was pillaging. To support them in combat, there was, in theory, a force of Turkish irregulars known as the bashi-bazouks. These men were no better than the slave trade soldiers they were supposed to fight. They were scattered over the place in small garrisons; each one spending much of its time slave hunting – without any hindrance from the rest. The people of Darfur detested and feared them. As upholders of Egyptian rule, they were useless. One of Gordon's first tasks would be to disband them, and to replace them with trustworthy Sudanese soldiers.

Strategically, his plan was to cut the slave traders off from their supplies of water, but this depended on an effective fighting force. It would have to wait, but he was not pessimistic. He would, he announced, overthrow Haroun without firing a shot. He would depend on the discontent of the local population, who discounted the rebel leader's claim to be the legitimate sultan of Darfur. He was, they thought, no better than Suleiman, the head of the slavers.

On 7 June, Gordon, wearing his field marshal's uniform, arrived at the frontier. He was riding one and a half hours ahead of his escort on an unusually athletic camel. 'I have,' he wrote afterwards, 'a splendid camel – none like it; it flies along and quite astonishes even the Arabs.' It certainly astonished the frontier post, where the soldiers were relaxing under the scorching desert sun, and not expecting any visitors. The infantry were still half asleep when he arrived, but the gunners had managed to scramble to their cannons and fire a ragged salute. Gordon waited until his escort had caught up, and then he pressed on to relieve the troops who were contained by Haroun's forces at Dara.

The rebellion was backed by Egyptians who had settled in Darfur, and were making a substantial living out of the slave trade. They wanted no interference from Cairo; and, as he passed through villages, Gordon was aware of a sullen, hostile, attitude. Safety lay on the other side of the frontier. This was enemy territory. At any moment, they might ride into an ambush. Well ahead of his troops again, Gordon rode alone, praying silently to himself, and reminded of the danger by the pain in his heart, which he had first experienced in Equatoria. It always came on in moments of peril. He was a man apart: most terribly alone. None of the escort could be trusted, and he had no Europeans on his staff. The faithful Gessi had been anxious to join him in Khartoum, but he had refused to give him a job. It was partly because the Italian had a family; and also that Gordon felt he had 'got very much too grand' (possibly on account of his successful exploration of Lake Albert). The two men quarrelled: Gessi threatened to publish the two hundred and fifty letters that Gordon had written to him. Gordon's reply was that 'it makes me laugh'. Who, he wondered, would be interested in reading them? Gessi's real crime, he suspected, was the recurring ailment of humanity – the need for applause.

Now, in this uncomfortable situation, he could no doubt have done with the reassuring presence of the Italian. He had ordered the troops at Dara to march out and meet him, but nobody came. His output of prayer increased, and it was not unrewarded. He reached the town without opposition, and set free 1,800 soldiers. He was now ready to march to El Fasher. But, before he could do that, one brief battle had to be fought against a tribe which was threatening the advance.

There was no doubt about it: Gordon had a considerable talent for drama. It was the small things, the casual gestures, which gave his men courage in desperate situations. When the fighting was at its peak, a spear thrown by one of the tribesmen narrowly missed him. Gordon did not even flinch: he calmly lit a cigarette – just as nonchalantly as if he were in the United Services Club. Then he looked critically about him. His men were firing wild, making a great deal of noise, but scoring far too few hits. He took a rifle from one of the soldiers, picked out the man who seemed to be the enemy leader, and carefully shot him through the heart. Then, with a murmured 'thank you', he handed the weapon back. The tribesmen, robbed of command, broke up. The engagement was over. Some while later, a friendly sheikh, who had been an interested spectator, recalled that he had never seen such a performance.

And then, on the following day, when he divided the spoil, no one was forgotten, and he kept nothing for himself. He was very tender-hearted about women and children, and never allowed them to be disturbed as is our custom in war; but he fed and clothed them at his own expense, and had them sent to their homes as soon as the war was over.

Gordon's skill at camel riding gained him considerable prestige among the population. 'It makes,' he wrote to Augusta, 'people fear me much more than if I were slow.' In some ways, his attitude reflected his measures against the Taipings in China: the forced marches, the sudden attacks which took the enemy by surprise. In China, however, he had The Ever Victorious Army to support him. In Darfur, he invariably arrived alone – with his somewhat euphemistically named 'escort' panting along in his wake – often many miles behind. When Dara was relieved, he likened the occasion to the relief of Lucknow. Once the troops at El Fasher had been freed, the rebellion in the north would be over. The brief battle at Dara had been sufficient to show the quality of the governor-general. The opposition melted away at El Fasher, and Haroun hurriedly departed for sanctuary in the mountains.

Meanwhile, however, Suleiman had left his base at Shakka in the south, and was said to be pillaging the neighbourhood three miles away from Dara. There was no time to consolidate his successes: Gordon had to be off. It was pointless to take the troops with him: they were still demoralized and obviously no match for Suleiman's reputedly ten-thousand-strong army of highly efficient native warriors. If he were to bring the slave trader to terms, Gordon would have to rely on his rapidly growing prestige and his personality. He could, as the sheikh said, be tender with the women and children, but his anger was worth a battery of fields guns. It was just as well, for it was his only weapon now. He set off with a party of fifty above-average bashi-bazouks, whom he affectionately referred to as 'my robbers'. With his phantom force, he intended to compel Suleiman to break up his army and to give up slave trading. Possibly Gordon's faith enabled him to believe in miracles: certainly nothing less than an enormous display of the supernatural could help him now. Optimist Gordon and Outraged Gordon had conferred with each other to stage a coup which was so far beyond reason that it might just conceivably, work.

As a piece of theatre, it was beautifully stage-managed. Shortly after dawn, Gordon led his 'robbers' to the enemy camp. The native warriors were paraded in two lines, as the young slave trader came out to meet him. He was, Gordon observed, 'a nice looking lad of twenty-two'. He may have been encouraged by rumours that Suleiman, too, had proposals to offer though any elation must have been quickly dispelled by a second suggestion. According to this report, everything depended on Suleiman's assessment of Gordon's forces. If they were overpoweringly strong, he would yield. If they were weak, he would annihilate them. One of the beauties of Gordon's plan was that it gave his young opponent no opportunity to make such an estimate. In the best tradition of bluff, he concealed his weakness; and, therefore, enabled it to be imagined as strength.

Gordon, playing the role of a governor-general making a routine inspection of his province, was wearing his uniform of 'golden armour'. There was little doubt in his mind that Suleiman was considering the idea of seizing him and holding him as hostage, and he was right. Fortunately, his sudden arrival had not given the young slave trader time to work out a plan. Instead, he ordered his artillery to fire a salute. It could either be taken as a respectful greeting, or as a threat.

With his small force of bashi-bazouks waiting outside the camp, Gordon, accompanied by his two secretaries, inspected the ranks of warriors. They were an impressive sight: 'smart, dapper troops,' he noted, 'like antelopes, fierce, unsparing, the terror of Central Africa.' Gordon of the *Boy's Own Paper* was living up to his role: he was even beginning to write like that magazine's contributors. Suleiman had only to give the signal, and his life would have been quickly ended. But, to see Gordon in his resplendent uniform, apparently cool beneath the scorching sun, relaxed, confident, even a little bit tetchy no one could have imagined his inner worries. A man who seemed to fear so little, they decided, must have had little to fear. Suleiman gave no signal to his men. These fit and aggressive black warriors stood firm – feeling, as soldiers everywhere feel, slightly self-conscious under the eye of an inspecting general.

Suleiman invited him to his tent and offered him refreshments. Gordon thanked him, and accepted a glass of water – nothing more. He refused to hold discussions on the spot, but instructed his host to come to Dara. They would talk matters over there, away from the menace of force which was still lined up outside. Suleiman agreed to come. Gordon put down the empty tumbler, beckoned to his secretaries and walked outside. He was helped on to the back of his camel and rode, almost contemptuously, back to Dara.

Throughout the day, there were discussions within the slave trader's camp. Some of the chiefs were in favour of using the occasion to complete the conquest of Darfur. By massacring the governor-general's forces, the Egyptian hold on the territory would be broken for ever. They could enjoy independence, and there would be no more talk of abolishing the slave trade. As for Gordon, he was only too well aware of this. At any moment, a massive cloud of dust might herald the advance of Suleiman's men. They never came. There was a brief meeting, when Suleiman and some of his chiefs came over to clarify the situation. Gordon's dialogue on this occasion was masterly. Somehow he managed to make his demands clear in an erupting mixture of broken Arabic, delicate gestures, and overpowering rage. Throughout the day, his opinion of Suleiman depreciated. The 'nice looking lad' became 'a poor little chap', who was soon to be replaced by 'the cub' who, when all was said and done, seemed to justify the opinion that 'a flogging would do him a lot of good'. It may have been true; but, on this occasion, Suleiman met most of the demands. Half of his army was to be incorporated into Gordon's force: he was allowed to take the remainder back with him to Shakka. He was to cease slave trading and submit to the rule of Egypt. The insurrection in Darfur was quelled – at any rate for the time being. Four weeks after he had set out, Gordon returned to Khartoum.

On the face of it, it seemed to have been a successful expedition, and it certainly reinforced the Khedive's impression that Gordon was a miracle worker. On the other hand, the two men responsible for the uprising were still at large, and one of them was back at his base with five thousand troops. It had been easy enough for Suleiman to agree to give up slave trading, for he must have realized that the demand could not be enforced. Short of total military occupation of Darfur, it was impossible to control matters outside the large towns. Six thousand other slave traders were also said to have thrown in their hands, when they heard about the submission of Zebehr's formidable son. But, here again, it was a question of making promises without the least intention of keeping them. At the best, Gordon's expedition, during which he covered two thousand miles by camel, could only be regarded as an effective piece of public relations. Haroun may have been holed up in the hills, but Suleiman would certainly come out fighting once things had settled down.

During this period, Gordon had given up alcohol. The action was partly in deference to his religious beliefs, and partly in sympathy for his liver. According to his own assessment, he slept better as a result – though the people in Cairo did little to improve his temper. By now the Anglo-Egyptian convention on the slave trade had taken place, and he was disappointed in the resolutions. There was no sense of urgency about them: they may have been drawn up with the idea of a more enlightened tomorrow – but, in one instance, this future was twelve years away. Gordon was more interested in the immediate present.

What was more, he was only too well aware that his mission could not be accomplished without a certain amount of ruthlessness. The Egyptian government was supposed to confer upon him the right to pass death sentences. This authority was never ratified: he had, as it were, to hang and be damned. He was a strange mixture. He could be generous beyond belief: an ardent practitioner of applied Christianity, who would go to immense trouble to help anybody in distress. But if his enemies imagined that his gentle disposition extended to Soldier Gordon – or, indeed, to Governor-General Gordon – they were making a dangerous mistake. When he felt events made it necessary, he could be very tough indeed. At least twice, he expressed himself happy at ordering the executions of rebel leaders who had surrendered. He disliked war, but he felt an even greater aversion for the men who caused it. Once, when he came across a slave convoy, he asked the boy in charge to tell him the owner's name. The lad hesitated. Gordon snatched his whip from him, and struck him across the face. It was, he admitted afterwards, 'cruel and cowardly'. But he was angry. He could not help it, he said. That seemed to be sufficient justification.

Shortly after his return to Cairo, he came to the conclusion that Darfur was too large and unruly a territory to be governed by remote control. It required somebody on the spot: preferably a European. He mentally flicked through his list of eligible people for the job, and decided that Sir Richard Burton was his man. As an explorer, Sir Richard had visited Mecca some twenty-four years previously in the disguise of a Moslem. This, surely, was by no means the least of his qualifications. He sent a letter to him at once, offering him the governorship. Sir Richard wrote back to say that he was now a family man, and needed rather more security than such a job could provide. But that was not his only reason for turning the offer down. 'You and I are too much alike,' he replied to Gordon. 'I could not serve under you, nor you under me.' After that, Gordon gave up the idea of a deputy, and tried to do the job as best he could from Khartoum.

The Khedive seemed to have such a high opinion of Gordon's abilities, that he considered no task impossible for him. In February 1878, he asked him to undertake the most improbable assignment of his career. The Egyptian debt had reached the hideous sum of £90 million. Now, the ruler decided, a commission should be appointed to investigate it. He asked Gordon to assume the role of president. He could not have chosen a more sympathetic person, for Gordon's own salary reflected the state of Egypt's finances. In Equatoria, he had been offered £10,000 a year, and he had accepted £2,000. The governor-generalship of the Sudan carried £12,000 a year, but he refused to take more than half that amount. More recently, he had cut this figure down to £3,000. It was partly an act of protest at the rewards of his fellow countrymen who were working in Cairo. As he remarked scathingly, he knew of one Englishman who had accepted £8,000 a year and a large home. 'He lived,' Gordon noted, 'in a style of luxury altogether inconsistent with the distressing condition of the country.' But such integrity did not mean that he was the man to solve Egypt's monetary crisis – quite the reverse, in fact. He had none of the deviousness, none of the diplomatic façade that was needed, and he was much too impatient. What was more, he had an intense dislike of the kind of life he would have to lead. 'The idea of dinners in Cairo makes me quail,' he told Augusta. 'I do not exaggerate when I say 10 minutes per diem is sufficient for all my meals, and there is no greater happiness to me than when they are finished.' None the less, his friend Khedive Ismail had sought his help. He should have it. Gordon was never one to turn a job down – even if he may have doubted his fitness for the proposed role. He packed a bag and went north to Cairo.

It is sometimes necessary to put a man into an improbable situation to discover the complete truth about him. The Gordon who emerged from the financial meetings in Cairo is a newcomer to this narrative. He is not the exulting theologian, so sure of his salvation, who appears in the letters to

Augusta; nor is he the practical and often ingenious soldier. As seen from his accounts of them, the negotiations in Cairo might well have provided the scenario for one of W. S. Gilbert's Savoy operas, and these writings were probably much nearer to the truth than the official reports. This is Gordon with an eye for the ridiculous, a deflator of pomposity, and a man it is very easy to like.

Nobody could accuse Gordon of not having done his homework. In 1875, he had discovered, Khedive Ismail had already been hopelessly in debt and groaning under the excessive interest demanded by his European creditors. He appealed to the government of the United Kingdom to send out a financier to advise him on what to do. The government, presumably in the belief that this was too difficult a problem for one man to tackle, sent out three. The trio decided that all the loans should be consolidated and that a lower rate of interest should be charged. In the following year, G. J. Goschen* was sent out to represent the English bondholders, whilst a man named Joubert, with a reputedly sharp eye for accountancy, was despatched on behalf of the French. As it turned out, these men were less astute than their reputations may have suggested. They carried out the job of consolidation, and recommended that the rate of interest should be cut by one per cent – which may have been fair enough. But they committed the fatal error of accepting the Khedive's figures without question. A child, with no more experience than that of negotiating pocket money, might have viewed with mistrust the labyrinthine methods of the ruler's book-keeping, but these two experts, either from idleness or lack of imagination, never questioned them.

But Goschen and Joubert were not the only prying financial eyes with return tickets to Egypt. Almost simultaneously, it was decided to set up a committee of four men to watch after the interests of all the creditors. Known as the Commissioners of Debt, they represented the four nations involved – Britain,

---

* Later First Viscount Goschen.

France, Germany and Austria. For all the good they did, this multiplicity of business brains might have stayed at home. By 1878, Khedive Ismail was unable to pay even the reduced rate of interest, and Egypt was virtually bankrupt. The salaries of the forces and the civil service had been unpaid for some considerable time. In desperation, Ismail asked for a further and more thorough inquiry. As he rightly deduced, however, such an investigation might cost him his sovereignty. After all, a chairman who has driven his company relentlessly into liquidation is unlikely to survive for long as chief executive. This, it seems, is why the ruler pleaded with Gordon to take on the job of president. He wanted to be sure that he had at least one friend in the reorganization and recriminations that were bound to ensue.

When Gordon arrived in Cairo on 7 March, he walked into a jungle of intrigue that was far more venomous than anything Equatoria had to offer. Ismail, not unreasonably, considered it unfair that the Commissioners of Debt should sit on the inquiry – and Gordon agreed with him. The commissioners, on the other hand, took the line that they should be present. There were mutterings in dark corners – with the ingenuous Gordon trying to apply his concept of economic justice in an atmosphere which, ethically, was little better than that of a Cairo bazaar. Ferdinand de Lesseps, who had been asked to assist him, turned out to be a man of straw, who wished for nothing better than to escape into the country with his nubile young wife. The British debt commissioner, Evelyn Baring, was a man to whom Gordon took an almost instant dislike, and his feelings for the British consul, H. C. Vivian, were not much warmer.

The climax came when Gordon decided what line of action the commission should take. Typically, he was on the side of the wretched Egyptian officials who had been unpaid for so long. What should be done, he said, was to suspend payment of the next instalment of interest, and to use the money on behalf of the state's employees. The Khedive could, he assured him, 'throw all blame upon me'. When he was told about it, His Highness seems to have been too overcome to discuss the matter. Making his excuses, he hurried away to his harem, where he shut himself up for two days. 'The game,' as Gordon all too rightly wrote, 'was lost.' It would all have been all right, Gordon felt sure, if only the Khedive Ismail had been prepared to *act* as a monarch; but he may have been over-confident. The British foreign minister, Lord Derby, also insisted that the debt commissioners should be present at the inquiry, and it was no use hoping that they would waive their countries' claims in favour of pay arrears for minor Egyptian functionaries. The cause was doomed.

When the Khedive eventually emerged from his harem, he would only talk about the Sudan to Gordon. 'His Highness,' he sadly observed, 'was bored with me after my failure and could not bear the sight of me.' The only thing to do was to resign which was, perhaps, just as well. The Khedive had not bargained on such a militant president. As Gordon was becoming uncomfortably aware, he had only been enlisted as a figure-head. It was better that somebody more familiar with the world of politics, and less concerned by the plight of the poor, should take over.

Five days later Gordon was on his way back to Khartoum – by ordinary train and paying his own passage. 'I calculate my financial episode cost me £800,' he wrote. He might have added that he had acquired, in return, an insight into the nature of political animals which might have availed him later – if only he had been able to realize it.

9

The End of an Assignment

Gordon was no match for the Commissioners of Debt and their masters; but he had, nevertheless, a talent for managing money. Just as he had turned Equatoria from a financial encumbrance into a profitable country, so was he able to halt the drain which the Sudan was making on Egypt's resources. In 1877, the country's expenditure had been £250,000 in excess of its revenue. In 1878, he reduced this figure to £70,000; and, in the following year, he broke even. Much of this was achieved by refusing to put into operation schemes which Khedive Ismail was eager to promote – but was in no position to undertake. There was, for example, an idea to build a Sudanese railway. It would have cost £750,000. Gordon said no. There was also a plan to construct two magnificent new river steamers – at a cost of £20,000. Again, Gordon, whose ideas on finance had a simplicity that would have delighted Mr Micawber, put his foot down.

For the nine months following his return from Cairo, he spent most of the time in his office. There were some triumphs: as, for instance, when his men captured twelve slave convoys in twelve months – setting free all the victims. There were also failures. Try as he would to fight the pernicious habit of graft, he was constantly receiving disappointments. He was compelled to dismiss eight senior army officers. Even the governor of Equatoria, whom he, himself, had groomed for promotion, was found to be guilty. Gordon's method of dealing with this man's crime was not according to any established law of jurisprudence. He tossed a coin. Before he did so, however, he asked God to make sure that it gave the right answer.

If it fell with the Sultan's cypher uppermost, the governor was to be shot. If it were not, his life would be spared. It landed cypher uppermost: the governor was arrested and put in chains. Unless God made a last-minute intervention, the sentence would be carried out. Luckily for the unhappy man, the Almighty decided to reverse the finding of the coin. The official was pardoned; but the experience must have caused him to repent, for he became one of Gordon's most loyal followers.

By July 1878, Gordon was able to report that he had produced 'a sort of government of terror'. If this seems to suggest the worst excesses of Nazi occupation or the French Revolution, he did himself much less than justice. The poor, the oppressed, even the underpaid soldiers, loved Gordon. If his ideas on justice seemed to depend on the toss of the coin, he was careful to see that this exercise in chance did not have the last word. God was always invited to intercede. Sometimes, it must be admitted, He was invited to play the role of devil's advocate!

Gordon's day began when he got up at seven o'clock each morning. He spent the period until luncheon giving interviews and reading petitions. During the afternoons, he had 'nothing particular to do' – which was just as well. The extreme heat made any activity difficult. Often he passed the time with his hobby of taking clocks to pieces and reassembling them. After dinner, he used to entertain guests for two hours. Then, he read for a bit and went to bed. Now and then, he complained of attacks of nausea, but these invariably yielded to Warburg's tincture – or, when this failed, to Dover's powders.

On one occasion, a party of missionaries passed through Khartoum on their way to Uganda. They called at the palace to pay their respects to the governor-general. The guard turned out to salute them: they were ushered upstairs, and

in a large corridor [one of them wrote] we saw a table laid for lunch, and a little man in his shirt sleeves walking about. I took him for the butler. On looking through the doors opposite I saw a very splendid divan. . . . But on catching sight of us the 'butler' rushed up and said, 'How d'ye do? So glad to see you! Excuse shirt sleeves. So hot! . . .' A hearty grasp of the hand to each, a piercing glance of small sharp eyes accompanied this flow of words, spoken in a clear, sharp but pleasant tone of voice. Yes, it is he indeed, the liberator of the slaves, the ruler of a country half as big again as France, the Chinese Gordon!

Another missionary noticed that he smoked a succession of fat cigars, which were rolled for him by one of his servants. Whenever he required a fresh one, he raised two fingers.

While Gordon was grappling with the tasks of administration in Khartoum, Suleiman the slave trader was making another attempt to seize power in Darfur. This young man has been likened to the Mahdi, though he had none of the latter's religious convictions. At their Dara meeting, Gordon had warned him never to make trouble again. If he did, the governor-general said, he would be ruined for ever. Unfortunately, Suleiman had not taken the advice seriously. Once again, he was supported by Arab colonists who were, as Gordon observed, 'still ready to seize the first chance of shaking off the yoke of Egypt'.

Suleiman's first action was to seize his father's old stamping ground at Bahr el Gazal. Gordon's problem was whom to put in charge of an expedition against him. He, himself, was too busy at Khartoum, and his local officers were not to be relied upon. By a happy chance, an old friend of Gordon's – the redoubtable Romolo Gessi – was in Khartoum at the time, fitting out an expedition to explore the Sobat River. Their quarrel had long since been forgotten and, when Gordon approached him, the Italian said that he would be only too happy to take command. It was a brave decision, for Suleiman's forces were estimated at 6,000, whilst all that Gordon could offer Gessi was a detachment of 300 regulars, plus 700 more or less useless irregulars, and two cannons. Still the cause was a good one. Apart from his territorial ambitions,

Suleiman had committed no fewer than 10,000 men, women and children to slavery in the previous six months – despite all his promises.

Gessi's offensive was delayed by rain and the need to train his troops. The Italian was frequently stricken by attacks of fever; he was once compelled to shoot two of his men who were attempting to incite a mutiny; and, after one engagement, his force was so short of ammunition, that his men had to pick up the bullets from the battlefield. His first success, however, was a tactical masterpiece. Suleiman and his army were installed in a fort surrounded by a double row of tree trunks. Within this compound, there was a strong point which was also Suleiman's residence. Gessi began with the traditional opening barrage, and his first shot was effective: it set fire to one of the wooden huts. The flames spread, until the whole fortress was ablaze. Suleiman and his men fled from the defences and ran into heavy rifle fire. The young slave trader escaped, but eleven of his chiefs and many more of his soldiers lay dead on the field. Unfortunately, Gessi was unable to follow up this triumph for, once again, his troops were running short of ammunition.

To expect Gordon to rest easy in his palace at Khartoum while out in the wilds a war was raging, was obviously asking too much. His health was bothering him at the time: the pain in the heart was becoming an uncomfortable commonplace – to such an extent, that he made a valiant attempt to give up smoking. 'If I had gone on with it much longer, I believe my heart would have stopped altogether,' he told Augusta. He never gave it up completely, but he was still refusing to drink brandy. 'Cognac is death to the liver, though I like it,' he said. 'I shall have no more for months.' Nevertheless, his ailments did not prevent him from setting off on 1,620-mile camel ride to bring reinforcements to Gessi. He took with him 250 men.

On their way to the rendezvous, they rounded up many slave caravans, and Gordon was appalled at the state of the victims. They had suffered most terribly. He reflected bitterly that, according to the law, the most severe punishment he could inflict on the dealers was to have them flogged and stripped of their possessions. As for the slaves, they were too far from home. He could only hand them over to the local tribe in the hope that they would be treated humanely. All this increased his anger at young Suleiman, who was the master mind behind this calculated brutality. When, at last, he reached Gessi, he was in no doubt about what instructions to give him. Suleiman was to be captured and shot. He handed his men over, and then set off back to Khartoum.

In spite of his losses, Suleiman still had a superior force to Gessi. The Italian, on the other hand, was a much better tactician and a pastmaster of cunning. The final encounter took place at daybreak on 16 July at a village named Gara – as Suleiman was fighting his way to join up with Haroun's rebels in the north. Gessi had concealed his troops in a wood. The respective sides were now: Suleiman, 900 men – Gessi, 300 men. But Suleiman had no way of guessing at the odds, for he could not see his opponent's troops. In fact, he thought there were many more of them. Consequently, when Gessi demanded his surrender within ten minutes, he meekly gave in. When, afterwards, he saw the size of the force ranged against him, he burst into tears. His soldiers were released on the promise that they would settle down and become respectable citizens. The 157 slave dealers on his establishment were chained together and sent off to prison. Suleiman and his ten chief supporters were shot on the spot. For his success in squashing the uprising, Gessi was rewarded with the rank of pasha and the sum of £2,000.

After Gordon had returned to Khartoum, his health seemed to worsen daily. His fears of angina became more serious, and he was troubled by frequent rushes of blood to the head. As he told Augusta, 'you think all is over. I have died suddenly over 100 times; but in these deaths I have never felt the least doubt of our salvation.' Before setting out on the expedition, he had refused three appeals from Khedive Ismail to go to Cairo. When he thought about his future, it was mostly to dream about retirement. His pension as a Royal

Engineer, he calculated, would bring him in £450 a year.

He had returned to the Sudanese capital in the early spring of 1879, so tired that he was consumed by a kind of frenetic energy which seemed to make him tireless. He found that Disraeli was still prime minister of England and that, with ample prodding from the British administration, Ismail had been deposed as Khedive.* He had been replaced by a younger man named Tewfik Pasha. Gordon's power in the Sudan was absolute. 'Not a man,' he wrote, 'could lift his hand without my authority.' But now, the time seemed to have come to relinquish it. What with his deteriorating health and Cairo politics, it was all too much. The British in the Delta were accusing him of being unpractical and, which was an even graver offence, *peculiar*. Some went so far as to share Disraeli's view that he was mad. With his friend Khedive Ismail now living in exile at Naples, he had no allies left. The slave trade would continue, aided by Egyptian ministers who had never, really, wanted to see an end to it. Gordon reached for a sheet of note paper, and wrote out his resignation. He then set off for Cairo, where he arrived on 23 August.

Somewhat to his surprise, he found that he liked the new Khedive. Before finally giving up his appointment, he told Tewfik that he had one more job to do. Trouble was still fermenting on the Abyssinian frontier. He considered it his duty to make some attempt to defuse the situation. The Khedive thankfully agreed. The less time that Gordon spent in Cairo, the better. He was, as the saying goes, political dynamite. Furthermore, if anyone could settle the Abyssinian question, it was he. The near-mad King Johannis had shown his feelings for the Egyptian ruler in a note which read as follows:

> Thank God, I and my soldiers are well. Is it to make peace you send me a letter? After having robbed me you have fought with me, without the knowledge of the kings [of Europe]. Why speak of peace while you stop the merchants

* Gordon disliked Disraeli intensely, and always insisted in spelling his name as D'Israeli, but this antipathy seems to have been mutual. Disraeli described a memorandum by Gordon on the Near East as the work of a 'madman'.

and arrest the people? The kings shall know my conduct and yours.

On the other hand, he was prepared to treat Gordon as a fellow christian whom he respected. His correspondence with him was in a much more pleasant vein.

I answer *you* [he wrote] on account of our friendship, my brother, also my brother in faith. Previously, I have told Moslems not to write to me, and as for me, I have not written any more to them. God will judge between Ismail Pasha and me. People without God have no good end.

It seems a strange coincidence that the only acceptable envoy to King Johannis was a heavy smoker. The king was so much against the habit, that he was apt to cut off the lips of those who indulged.

Tewfik gave Gordon two sets of instructions for his mission: one of them written in Arabic, and the other in French. As he travelled along the mountain tracks towards the Abyssinian capital, however, Gordon became more and more convinced that it was a useless errand. Even with him as a mediator, King Johannis would not treat with the Khedive of Egypt. He would insist that nothing could be settled without the intervention of 'the kings', by which he really meant the English and French governments. Boils were now added to Gordon's other physical torments: his temper became worse, and he began to imagine tortuous intrigues by Tewfik. 'I believed,' he afterwards recalled, 'that it was hoped that something not over-agreeable would happen to me through the king, and thus England would get mixed up in the dispute.' As things turned out, he was right about the need for French and British intervention. Johannis demanded £2 million, or, alternatively, the Italian port of Masawah, as the price of peace on the frontier. It was out of the question. After a great deal of discomfort and some humiliation, Gordon returned to Cairo – where he found that his enemies had been feeding British newspaper men with reports calculated to harm his reputation.

One of them was taken up by *The Standard* in London.

At a council of ministers held at Cairo, at which the European controllers were present, [the newspaper told its readers] a dispatch was read from Colonel Gordon, saying that £250,000 of taxes remained uncollected in the Sudan; that the ministers were surprised at this, and that Tewfik had demanded an explanation from Gordon.

A later report from the paper's man in Cairo said:

Gordon, in another dispatch, desires to cede to Italy a Port in the Red Sea, in order to produce complications on the part of Italy and Abyssinia. The ministers were unanimous in rejecting the proposal; other despatches of Gordon were read, which showed his inconsistency.

The Egyptian newspapers were more direct. According to Gordon, they 'contained a number of small paragraphs, saying that I was mad, and refused to obey orders'. What should have been one of the high points in his career, the culmination of all his efforts, which had overcome two rebellions in Darfur, made the Sudanaese budget balance, and had resulted in his winning the love of his people, was now kicked into the gutter by the smears of the press. No wonder Gordon seemed to be becoming eccentric. The only thing to do was to go home.

Vivian had been posted to Brussels as British ambassador and his post as consul-general in Cairo had been taken over by Edward Malet. As a reward for his services, Vivian had been invested with the CB, and the award was discussed at a gathering at which Gordon happened to be present. One of the guests, Nubar Pasha, made what Gordon considered to be a disparaging remark about Vivian. To the Egyptian's considerable surprise, he heard Gordon challenge him to a duel on the following morning. As the latter told Malet, 'I will not permit anyone to speak in such a way of a man who belongs to the same Order of Knighthood as I do.' It was left to the unfortunate Malet to calm Gordon down by extracting a grudging apology from Nubar Pasha.

Before leaving for home, Gordon visited a doctor in Alexandria for a check-up. He was found to be suffering from nervous exhaustion and an 'alteration of the blood'.* Several months of rest were prescribed 'with no business or political excitement'. He sailed for England on 10 January 1880, stopping at Naples (where he lunched with the exiled Ismail), and at Rome (where the wonders of St Peter's failed to impress him). By 2 February, he was staying with Augusta at Southampton: ill, out of work, and with no honours to show for his services to the Sudan and Equatoria. He was living proof that virtue is only rewarded when it is backed by the Establishment.

However, as a final word on this phase of his career, *The Times* had something nice to say about him. 'All true friends of civilization will regret his departure (from the Sudan),' the paper's leader writer observed. And Gordon was quoted as saying: 'I do not profess to have been either a great ruler or a great financier, but I can say this, I have cut off the slave-dealers in their strongholds, and I have made all my people love me.' Such a claim was so uncharacteristic, that one wonders whether it was the product of his nervous exhaustion, or else an attempt to fight back at his critics. *The Times* explained that slavery could be overcome only by a continuous struggle, and then only 'by a combination of qualities such as we can hardly hope to find in Colonel Gordon's successor, whoever he may be'. As things turned out, the newspaper was disturbingly right. The official who was appointed to take his place was an unsavoury character named Raouf Pasha – whom Gordon had twice dismissed for corruption. The plans for exploiting Equatoria were abandoned, and everything resumed its unprogressive normality, which pleased the statesmen and the financiers and the merchants, but would have broken Gordon's heart. He might just as well have never been near the place.

* Despite his worries, there was never any medical evidence to show that he suffered from angina pectoris – though he appears to have had a serious liver condition latterly.

10
The Empty Years

Gordon's last action as governor-general of the Sudan (1877-80 version) took place in Lausanne. It was recorded by a clergyman, The Rev R. H. Barnes, who was staying at the same hotel. Mr Barnes had noticed 'an English gentleman', accompanied by a youngster, who occupied a corner table in the dining room. He was a man 'of middle height, very strongly built; his face was furrowed with deep lines; and his fine broad brow and most determined mouth indicated a remarkable power of grave and practical thought.' The stranger fell into conversation with him, and one day invited him to his room. Mr Barnes noticed some documents on the table. 'You have been in Palestine and know Arabic,' his companion said. 'Look at those papers.'

> I took several of them in my hand and glanced at them, [Mr Barnes continues] but soon laid them down, remarking that I knew very little Arabic. 'They are Death Warrants,' he said. I was so startled that I exclaimed, 'Death warrants! why, who are you?' 'Don't you know me?' he answered; 'I have been Governor-General of the Sudan and still nominally retain the position; but nothing now remains for me but to sign these papers – that will end it.'

His trip to Switzerland had been partly to restore his health; but, more specifically, on behalf of the youngster who was with him at the hotel. The lad was one of his late brother's sons, and they had been investigating schools. Gordon considered it a useful idea that some of the children's education should take place abroad. Since he would almost certainly be paying the school fees, there was no one to argue with him.

The enforced rest, like most of Gordon's leisure, had been uncomfortable. When he visited Augusta, he spent most of his time in the kitchen; for, in spite of his good resolutions, he was smoking very heavily indeed, and this was the only room in which his tyrannical sister permitted it. He was full of depression about himself and the Establishment. He described himself in a letter to Sir Richard Burton's wife, as 'an orb which is setting, or rather is set'; and he lamented about 'a great Government like ours governed by men who dare not call their souls their own'. In Whitehall, he was unpopular 'for I have writen hard things to them'. Elsewhere, however, he was socially very desirable – if only he would accept invitations. At his sister-in-law's house in Kensington, he was reputed to crawl underneath the table when visitors called. He even had the temerity to decline an invitation to a banquet given by the Prince of Wales. His excuse was that he always went to bed at half past nine. The Prince, who was by no means insensitive to his feelings, invited him, instead, to an informal luncheon on the following Sunday. Gordon accepted. Among the other guests was the Duke of Cambridge, who advised him to take at least a year's leave.

On his way to Switzerland, he had stopped off at Brussels to discuss with King Leopold ways of suppressing the slave trade in the Congo. Otherwise, for most of the time, he was bored. As he said, 'inaction is terrible to me'. An offer from the governor of the Cape Colony in South Africa to take over the command of the colonial forces at a 'supposed salary' of £1,500 a year was turned down. He gave no reason, though it was certainly not the pay. Possibly, he did not feel fit enough yet. The time dragged tediously on. In April 1880, W. E. Gladstone replaced Disraeli as head of the government. With the former opposition party in power, Gordon's prospects for the future might improve – though he expected little enough from it. 'I am,' as he told one friend, 'already dead.'

One afternoon in May, he was walking in London with his brother Henry, when they noticed a hansom cab drawn up outside the latter's house. The occupant was a messenger from the Marquis of Ripon, who had recently been appointed viceroy of India. The Marquis wanted to know whether Gordon would go with him as his private secretary. Surprisingly, he agreed. Two weeks later, he was on his way to Bombay via Brindisi.

Lord Ripon could hardly have made a less suitable choice. Gordon had accepted the position in what he later admitted to be 'a moment of weakness'. Once he reached Bombay, he saw, as he had already expected, that he could do nothing 'in the face of vested interests out there'. He already knew that his views were 'diametrically opposed to those of the official classes' – unless he was careful, this was going to be Cairo all over again. But the experience in Egypt had not been entirely wasted. At least he had learnt to notice the symptoms of such a situation. Within a week of his arrival in India, he had handed the viceroy his resignation. He even offered to repay the money for his passage (which was accepted!). He had 'ratted', he said, 'so as to hurt Lord Ripon very little. We left the best of friends.'

There he was, then, without a job and almost penniless in Bombay. But somebody, either temporal or spiritual, must have been watching him. Two days after his resignation, he received an urgent invitation to return to China. The country was, it seemed, on the verge of war with Russia, and Gordon's advice was needed. A frantic exchange of telegrams with the Horse Guards followed. From Gordon: 'Obtain me leave until end of the year; never mind pay; am invited to China; will not involve Government.' From the Horse Guards to Gordon: 'Must state more specifically purpose and position for and in which you go to China.' Gordon to Horse Guards: 'Am ignorant; will write from China before the expiration of my leave.' Horse Guards to Gordon: 'Reasons insufficient; your going to China is not approved.' Gordon to Horse Guards: 'Arrange retirement, commutation or resignation of service. . . . My counsel, if asked, would be for peace, not war. I return by America.' On the day he wrote the last telegram, he embarked in a cargo steamer for Hong Kong. When the vessel called at Ceylon, he found another message waiting for him. It told him that his leave would be granted – on the condition that he would undertake no military service in China. Gordon reassured the authorities, though everybody seems to have overlooked the fact that he was still – by title at any rate – a field marshal in the Chinese army.

Fourteen years had passed since his service with The Ever Victorious Army, but some of his old friends were on the dock to greet him, when the steamer came alongside at Hong Kong. Quincey, the baby he had taken care of at Quinsan, now had a wife and three children. Lar Wang's son was a mandarin. From time to time, Gordon had corresponded with Li Hung Chang from Khartoum. The affair of the murdered Taiping leaders was forgiven, if not forgotten. He and Li were again the best of friends, and Gordon assumed that this sudden call from China had been a diplomatically disguised plea for help from Li. The advice he would give had already been released to the world in a statement of policy he had made before leaving India. 'Inclined as I am, with only a small degree of admiration for military exploits,' he had written, 'I esteem it a far greater honour to promote peace than to gain any paltry honours in a wretched war.'

The British authorities regarded Gordon as the country's most dangerous export – and never more so than when he visited a nation with such a talent for intrigue as China. Currently, the ruling powers were up to their exalted necks in this favourite pastime; and, unless they were careful, the outcome would be a thrashing by the Russians. The British ambassador was charged with responsibility for keeping Gordon quiet – or, at least, keeping him out of trouble. As things turned out, there was little he could do, for Gordon never set foot inside the legation throughout his visit. Most of his time was spent at Li Hung Chang's palace at Tientsin. It was not, however, Li who was responsible for his coming – but, strangely enough, Li's opponents in the government.

China's government was divided on the question of war

with Russia. The Doves, as one might say, were headed by Li: the Hawks, by a militant member of the Manchu dynasty named Prince Chun. As if to complicate the situation, the German ambassador had blundered on the scene with an idea that Li should march to Peking with his so-called 'Black Flag' army; depose the Emperor; and seize power. An international war would be averted, though the German minister does not seem to have considered that the probable result would have been a civil war with equally disastrous results.

When he arrived at Li's palace, Gordon was asked what he thought of the German Plan.

> I told him [he wrote] that I was equal to a good deal of filibustering, but that this was beyond me, and that I did not think there was the slightest chance of such a project succeeding, as Li had not a sufficient following to give it any chance of success.

What, then, could be done? Did this mean that war with Russia was inevitable? Gordon said that he hoped not. He would go to Peking and talk to Chun and his followers. It was a dangerous undertaking. He had been warned by the British minister that, if he valued his life, he should not make his presence known in the capital. Gordon did not set a high price on his existence, but that was beside the point. He had work to do. The question was whether or not Chun and his lieutenants would listen to him, for he was about to tell them things they would not like.

Gordon's audience, which consisted of members of the Grand Council, were waiting for him. A nervous interpreter became even more so as the conversation proceeded. At one point, the unfortunate man accidentally knocked over a cup of tea. Gordon began by pointing out that the Russians were by far the stronger of the two powers. They could, at any moment, swoop down on Peking, capture the city without difficulty, and then dictate their own terms. Very well, the ministers said, what would he advise? The first thing to do, Gordon explained, was to burn down all the suburbs of the city, and to build proper fortifications in their place. At the same time, they should remove the Emperor to a place of safety. If they did that, he would stay and help them. Otherwise, it was no use even considering war: Peking was much too exposed.

But surely, the ministers objected, there were the Taku forts at the mouth of the river? They were very strong. Gordon replied that they were certainly effective at the front; but anyone who cared to make the necessary diversion could attack them easily enough from the rear. In any case, he happened to know that they had insufficient stocks of rice to keep the garrison supplied with food for any length of time. The conversation went backwards and forwards, with Gordon becoming increasingly angry. At one point, the interpreter refused to continue – he was too afraid for his own safety. Gordon picked up an English-Chinese dictionary he found on the table, thumbed through it quickly, and then pointed to a word. It was: 'idiocy'.

Having established his point that China was in no state to win a war, Gordon then dictated what he considered would be acceptable terms for peace. There were five articles in all. The only one the Grand Council objected to was the fifth, which was concerned with the payment of money.

They said this was too hard and unjust [Gordon wrote]. I said that might be, but what was the use of talking about it? If a man demanded your money or your life, you have only three courses open: you must either fight, call for help, or give up your money. Now, as you cannot fight, it is useless to call for help, since neither England nor France would stir a finger to assist you. I believe these are the articles under discussion at St. Petersburg, and the only one on which there is any question is the fifth.

He was right. What is more, his arguments prevailed. By the middle of August, peace was assured, and Li was back in power again. Before he left China, Gordon wrote his final testament for the Chinese. One paper dealt with what the country should do in the event of being attacked. The other had to do with more general matters concerning the nation's reconstruction. The former appeared some time afterwards in a modified form as an article on guerilla warfare, which was published in the *Army and Navy Gazette*. If the British generals had studied it more carefully, they might have brought the Boer War to a much quicker conclusion.

Among the points which Gordon made were that China's strength lay in her large population and in the mobility of her troops. The needs of the latter were simple: they required little baggage. The country's forces should never become engaged in pitched battles. They should make their attacks at night-time, but they should not push them home. A lightning strike – and then an equally rapid withdrawal: the idea was to worry the enemy continuously. Rockets, he said, should replace cannons, and no artillery should accompany the forward troops. It would merely delay them. In any case, he said, infantry was by far the more lethal. 'Guns make a noise far out of proportion to their value in war,' he wrote. Finally, so long as Peking was the capital, China should never become engaged in a war with any first-class power. It was far too close to the sea. For much of the document, he was putting down the lessons he had learned, all those years ago, with The Ever Victorious Army.

His civil memorandum encouraged China to concentrate on the electric telegraph and canals for her communications. Railways were far too costly. As he knew from bitter experience, they had ruined Egypt. He urged the government to improve its diplomatic representation abroad – and to give its businessmen economic aid for the building of factories in England to produce their own cotton goods. The idea was to cut out the middle men who were systematically taking the cream off China's milk. Whether from opposition by the British, or indolence from the Chinese, it was never adopted.

While he was writing this, he received a telegram from the Horse Guards to the effect that his leave had been cancelled and that he should return home immediately. Nobody seemed to be particularly impressed by the fact that he had just prevented a major war. He had been thinking of visiting Zanzibar on the way back, but now he changed his plans. It was, perhaps, about time he looked in on the War Office. He reached Southampton on 21 October, just before the publications of his letters from the Sudan, which had been edited by Dr Birbeck Hill. Not that the occasion gave him any pleasure: he had only consented to their being printed on the condition that any references which might seem to reflect credit on himself should be removed – and that a tribute should be paid to his secretary, Berzati Bey. Beyond saying that, he wanted nothing to do with the project. He refused to see Dr Hill – telling him to treat matters as if he were already dead. The task of negotiating with the editor was left to his brother Henry.

Gordon was determined not to board 'the tram of the world'. Nevertheless, he did have what he might have considered to be one lapse. After a great deal of persuasion from the magazine's editor, he agreed to pose for a cartoon to be published in *Vanity Fair*. The text which appeared beside it might have been specially written for those chicken-hearted officials and ministers, who seemed to be incapable of appreciating Gordon's genius.

He was, the editorial said,

the most conscientious, simple-minded and honest of men. He has a complete contempt for money, and after having again and again rejected opportunities of becoming rich beyond the dreams of avarice, he remains a poor man, with nothing in the world but his sword and his honour. The official mind, being incapable of understanding this, regards it as a sign of madness. And as it is found that besides being utterly without greed he is also entirely without vanity or self-assertion, he is set down by the officials as being 'cranky' and unsafe to employ . . . He is very modest and very gentle, yet full of enthusiasm for what he holds to be right. This enthusiasm often leads him to interfere in

165

matters which he does not understand, and to make in haste statements he has to correct at leisure. But he is a fine, noble, knightly gentleman, such as is found but once in many generations.

There have been few better portraits of Charles Gordon than this.

PART III

The Victim

11
The Fruitless Search

The documents which Gordon had left behind him in China were, in a sense, a situation report of his civil and military outlook in his forty-eighth year. The memorandum on defence propounded a philosophy that might have been expected from the commander of The Ever Victorious Army. The long homily on the country's reconstruction clearly came from the pen of the ex-governor-general of the Sudan. His experiences in Equatoria and at Khartoum had given him a new appetite – which had not, strangely enough, been blunted by his unfortunate interlude in Cairo. If a saint had hovered in the background of Soldier Gordon, that individual was now accompanied by another figure. Gordon had acquired a taste for government – without developing any liking for its concomitant trade of politics. Perhaps he saw himself as a roving trouble-shooter: an administrator whose mission came neither from the Whigs nor the Tories, whose leaders he detested with impartiality, but direct from the Almighty.

Throughout most of his life, he had been an avid reader of newspapers.

On his return from China, he came across a pamphlet written by a Mr Tuke. It described in outraged and poignant terms the plight of the peasants in Ireland. Did he link them in his mind with the 'scuttlers' of Gravesend? And did he believe that he might be able to devise a solution to a problem which had baffled both the English and the Irish for a great many years? At all events, under the guise of taking a shooting holiday, he set off for Bantry in the late autumn of 1880. His real, and unprofessed, object was to find out more about the lower Irish orders who inhabited hovels over in the west.

As he might have expected at this time of year, the weather was vile. Beneath dripping skies he strode over the hills, peering into dim recesses of human habitation, appalled at the situation and indignant at the apparent indifference that had produced it. On 1 December, he sat down and wrote a long letter to his old friend, Colonel John Donelly. Donelly was a fellow sapper: the two men had served together at Sebastopol, and the amiable officer had often acted as a sounding board for Gordon's opinions. When he received the long note about Ireland, he decided that it merited a more substantial readership. He promptly sent it on to the editor of *The Times*, who printed it two days later. That newspaper and the *Pall Mall Gazette* both published leading articles about it.

There was nothing particularly new about his ideas, but Gordon had an instinctive flair for producing newspaper copy. The villains of the piece, as anyone who had given even a cursory glance to the situation must have known, were the landlords. 'A gulf of antipathy,' Gordon wrote, 'exists between [them] and tenants of the north-west, west, and south-west of Ireland. It is a gulf which is not caused alone by the question of rent; there is a complete lack of sympathy between these two classes.' The only solution, he suggested, was to get rid of the former. The government should buy up the greater part of Longford, Westmeath, Clare, Cork, Kerry, Limerick, Lietrim, Sligo, Mayo, Cavan, and Donegal. The owners should receive adequate compensation: thereafter, the counties should be administered by a Land Commission, which would also make provision for the time-honoured remedy for distressed Irishmen – emigration.

The state of our fellow-countrymen in the parts I have named is worse than that of any people in the world, let alone Europe [he wrote]. I am not well off, but I would offer ———— [unnamed, but presumably an Irish landlord] or his agent £1,000, if either of them would live one week in one of these poor devils' places, and feed as these people do.

The offer was not accepted: the government took no heed of the advice, and the War Office doubtless chalked up another black mark on the record of an officer who was showing a disturbing tendency to think – and, therefore, to become eccentric.

However, *The Freeman's Journal* of Dublin was ecstatic, and labelled Gordon 'one of the most remarkable men of our own or any time'. *The Standard*, which was inclined to be lukewarm about his excursions into the jungle of government, was less enthusiastic. Its leader writer dismissed the letter as 'the experience of a superficial glance at the disquieted island'.

The Gordon of this period might be seen as a missionary without a cause. Nobody seemed anxious to employ him: he was worried about the lot of his fellow men, and restless at his inability to do anything about it. He once observed that 'my object has been always to put myself into the skin of those I may be with.' That was all very well: there was no better way of discovering the truth. Nevertheless, it did not conform with the image of Victorian imperialism. The country ruled a huge section of the globe, but the rulers were not encouraged to identify with the subject populations. The place for authority was above and apart from the local inhabitants. You did not, for example, find the ex-patriate Englishmen in Cairo rubbing shoulders with the fellaheen.

Having tasted the experience of contributing to a newspaper, Gordon followed up his piece about Ireland with a letter on the points for and against maintaining a garrison in Afghanistan. Although he had never been there, he had put himself sufficiently 'into the skin' of the tribesmen to observe that 'they prefer their own bad native governments to a stiff, civilized government, in spite of the increased worldly prosperity the latter may give.' The only point in occupying the country was to shut the gate which might admit the Russians to India. Such a course, he believed, would be a mistake.

Politically, militarily, and morally, Kandahar ought not to be retained [he wrote]. It would oblige us to keep up an interference with the internal affairs of Afghanistan, would increase the expenditure of impoverished India, and expose us chronically to the reception of those painfully sensational telegrams of which we have had a surfeit of late.

His letter appeared in *The Times* on 22 February 1881. Four days later, the *Army and Navy Gazette* printed his article on guerilla warfare. Much of it was along the lines of the memorandum he had written for the Chinese, but it contained one passage which the authorities would have done well to note.

The individual man [he wrote] of any country in which active outdoor life, abstinence, hunting of wild game, and exposure to all weathers are the habits of life, is more than a match for the private soldier of a regular army, who is taken from the plough or from cities, and this is the case doubly as much when the field of operations is a difficult country, and when the former is, and the latter is not, acclimatized.

It was almost a preview of the Boer War.

The joy of writing began to wane. Gordon relapsed into boredom. Florence Nightingale told him that he should go back to India. The government would never have agreed to his going; and, in any case, he was no better equipped than he had been to endure the rigours of the British Raj. He noticed references in the papers to troubles in Basutoland, and remembered the offer from the Cape government. Perhaps this would give him the outlet he needed? He sent off a telegram, saying 'Gordon offers his services for two years, at £700 per annum, to assist in terminating the war, and administering Basutoland.' It was presumably, delivered to the appropriate desk, but whoever received it never gave him the courtesy of a reply.

Nobody, it seemed, wanted him. For want of any better occupation, he became uneasily aware, it might be necessary to go back to regimental soldiering in the Royal Engineers. The thought apalled him. Intellectually and in status, he had outgrown this sort of thing, and it was bound to be disastrous. 'For myself,' he told a friend, '(*in re* this forced employment in the obstructive circle of RE) duty was particularly vexatious, for I should certainly have come to dire loggerheads with my obstructive RE chiefs.' In the end, all that remained was a sickly lozenge of land in the Indian Ocean named Mauritius to which, on 4 May, he was appointed Chief Royal Engineer.

Gordon left London on 4 May, travelling via Le Havre, where bad news was waiting for him. A telegram announced that Romolo Gessi had recently died in Aden. The Italian was, it seemed, literally worn out by his work among impossible people in an impossible climate. 'How I warned him to leave with me!' Gordon commented. He proceeded sadly on his way to what promised to be very unexciting work in an unpleasant place.

During his residence in Mauritius, Gordon wrote three papers – each of which was a very clear-headed analysis of its subject. One of them was a study of Egyptian affairs since Ismail had been deposed as Khedive. The second was a report on coaling stations in the Indian Ocean, and the third was a discussion on the relative merits of the Suez Canal and the Cape of Good Hope as routes to India and the Far East. Gordon took the view that the latter was best. He mistrusted the Suez Canal as unreliable. As he pointed out, a dredger had recently gone out of control and blocked the channel with chaotic results. If one, comparatively small, vessel could produce such havoc, the canal's potential for disaster was enormous.

On 24 March 1882, he was promoted to major-general and made commandant of all the troops on the island. Less than a month later, a telegram from Mr Merriman, the Cape Colony's prime minister reached him. 'Position of matters in Basutoland grave,' the premier had written, 'and it is of the utmost importance that colony should secure the services of someone of proved ability, firmness, and energy.' He repeated the offer which had been made two years previously, when Gordon was taking a holiday in Switzerland – though, he emphasized, he did 'not expect [him] to be bound by the salary then stated'. The Colonial Office and the War Office had, it seemed, agreed to the appointment. Gordon accepted with alacrity and set off immediately for Grahamstown in a sailing ship named the *Scotia*.

It was a shocking journey. High seas battered the tired timbers of the ancient *Scotia*, and adverse winds added days to the passage. For four weeks, Gordon suffered the agony of seasickness with a brave, if green, face until at last, in early May, he thankfully disembarked at Cape Town. On 26 May, he reached Grahamstown.

Gordon might be considered a man whose demands from life were very moderate. He asked for little in the way of monetary rewards, and one might have expected that, whatever storms assailed the rest of his turbulent existence, financial matters would not be among them. But nothing, for a man of his type, is ever simple. In the case of his present appointment, the Cape government had agreed to a salary of £1,200 a year – plus £300 a year expenses. It was, in all conscience, little enough to pay a man who was being asked to get the country out of a war which had already cost it £4 million. Nevertheless, true to the Gordon form, he insisted that it was too much. He would only accept £800, though he did demand that the balance should be spent on providing him with a secretary. In fact, his generosity was not quite so great as it may have seemed, for he had counted on receiving a further £500 a year from the British government as 'Imperial Pay' – in other words, a special allowance for officers and men who policed and patrolled those sprawling splotches of pink, which marked the British Empire on maps of the world.

While he was stationed on Mauritius, Gordon had been out of touch. Among the details of army life which had escaped the island was a directive passed in June 1881, modifying the situation and making it clear that a general officer employed by a colonial government would receive no such grant. He protested, but the authorities refused to budge. If any extra money was required, they said, the Cape Colony should pay it. Gordon pointed out that it was not the colony's responsibility, and that he had no intention of making such a request. Eventually, the argument wore itself out from sheer inertia – though Gordon nursed a sense of injustice. It was not, he would have pointed out, that he cared a jot for the extra £500: it acted as an affront to his sense of what was right and what was wrong.

If anyone were looking for portents of ill at the outset of his mission to the Cape, the financial question would have been a good starting point. Another small, if fruitful, field of research would have been a dinner given in his honour by the governor of the Cape. It began badly, by his stepping on the train of the governor's wife, Lady Robinson. Throughout dinner, he said what turned out to be the wrong things; and, when leaving, he addressed her as 'Lady Barker'. It was a mere piece of absentmindedness, but Lady Barker happened to be a person whom Lady Robinson detested. Gordon could hardly wait to meet the Basutos. Whatever strange rituals they might observe would be child's play compared with the tribal customs of the white population in Cape Town.

His assignment might have been made easier if the government in the colony had not been in the process of changing hands. Mr Merriman, the prime minister who believed in seeking an humane accommodation with the Basutos, was being replaced by Mr Scanlen, who did not. Nor was the situation helped by the latter's choice of a secretary for native affairs. The role was filled by an unlikeable individual named Suar, whose policy was evidently to divide and rule. If it were carried out effectively, the Basutos might cease to be a problem by the simple act of destroying themselves.

Gordon never skimped his research. As secretary, he had obtained the services of an excellent army officer named Colonel Ffolliott; and, with Ffolliott's help, he delved into the roots of the Basutoland troubles. The results were not

175

encouraging, and reflected small credit on the colony's government. The country had, it seemed, a population of about 150,000 who lived in a self-sufficient mountainous area – cut off from the Cape by the Drakensberg range. In 1845, the limits of Basutoland had been recognized by Her Majesty's government; and, three years later, the chiefs had agreed to accept the sovereignty of the Queen on the strict understanding that they would keep to their side of the Drakensbergs, and the British settlers should keep to theirs. In spite of these treaties, the ability of the Basutos to govern themselves, and to preserve their own state, was steadily eroded. There were wars, and a further litter of broken pledges by the British until, in 1880, a serious attempt was made to disarm the tribesmen. Not unnaturally, they resented it. The British claimed that they had prevented the country from being absorbed by the Boers by giving it their protection. It was, they said, all very unfair. With self-righteousness spurring both of them on, the two sides went to war again.

Gordon and Ffolliott ploughed their ways through a mass of verbiage, and presently uncovered a situation which more than explained the recurring conflict which had been so costly to the Cape government.

The fault [Gordon was to write] lay in the British Government not having consulted the Basutos, their co-treaty power, when they handed them over to the Colonial Government. They should have called together a national assembly of the Basuto people, in which the terms of the transfer could have been quietly arranged, and this I consider is the root of all the troubles, and expenses, and miseries which have sprung up.

Like so many instances of quarrels between overdogs and underdogs, it really amounted to a failure to communicate. Gordon, who was a great communicator, believed that 'it would be as well to let bygones be bygones, and to commence afresh by calling together by proclamation a [meeting] of the whole tribe, in order to discuss the best means of sooner

176

securing the settlement of the country.' The outcome, he had no doubt, would be a Basuto assembly, empowered to voice the natives' grievances. They would be given semi-independence, with a British resident to look after their external affairs. All this he wrote down in an impressive report, admirably lucid and providing a constructive picture of the situation, which he presented to Mr Scanlen. The new premier, presumably read it: if he did, however, he failed to adopt any of Gordon's recommendations.

At the same time, Gordon had been asked to draw up a plan for the reorganization of the Cape's armed forces. The government, apparently, had asked him 'to peel red tape off the colonial system', which was a task he was more than qualified to carry out. 'I do hate,' he told his friend John Donelly, 'our complicated system with which we are so completely satisfied.' Once he had completed his investigation, he produced a scheme by which the colony could support an army of four thousand men for no more money than it had cost to employ one thousand. It meant of course, that some people would have to go – and that there would have to be economies, which would cut holes in a number of influential pockets. It also meant an end to a system in which officers, who were insubordinate in peacetime, could not be punished 'for political reasons'. Of those – and there were many – who opposed this overhaul of the forces, nobody was more against it than prime minister Scanlen. It had not been, as he no doubt pointed out, his idea to hire Gordon; but that of his predecessor, Mr Merriman. Although there is no record of his saying it, it became quite obvious that he had decided Gordon's usefulness was at an end. To effect his removal without loss of credit to himself, he relied on the support of his colleague – the secretary for native affairs – in other words, the devious Mr Suar.

Much of Gordon's comparatively brief stay in the Cape Colony was spent at a desk, composing reports. He got on well with Ffolliott, who received the full force of many highly evangelical arguments without succumbing to them completely. He now, according to his mentor, 'receives the truth', but he never graduated to the point 'of looking on death as life'. In a lesser matter, Gordon was more successful. He disliked it when Ffolliott insisted on addressing him as 'Sir'. To discourage this habit, he put a collecting box in the office. Every time the colonel used the word, he had to put 1s. 0d. into it. He had contributed 15s. 0d. to goodness knows what charity before he was finally cured of the habit.

The Boer settlers, Gordon had decided, were a natural target for his religious messages. Consequently, he had some of the tracts which he had used at Gravesend translated into Dutch. Augusta was asked to send out a supply. On his walks, he left copies beside the roads in the vicinity of farms. He had no means of finding out how successful they were; for, in the meanwhile, Mr Suar had concocted a plot which, he felt confident, would dispose of Gordon and the Basuto problem at one and the same time. If any award were given for double-dealing villainy at its most adroit, the knavish Suar would have been a prime contender for it.

Gordon was now living at King William's Town, where the depot for the Cape forces was situated. One day, Suar turned up, and asked him to keep him company on a journey to Basutoland. Gordon refused at first: he could not see what good it would do. However, the secretary of native affairs suggested that it might be beneficial, if he visited a chief named Masupha. Masupha was a difficult man, and a discussion might help to clear the air. Gordon agreed – provided he was only accompanied by his private secretary and two servants. The informal approach would be seen as an act of friendship.

While Gordon was travelling through the mountains, Suar was on his way to a different part of the province, where he persuaded another chief to attack Masupha's territory. His theory was that the two tribes would annihilate each other. As for Gordon, he would be in the worst of all possible worlds, for Masupha would regard the invasion as treachery by a man who had enjoyed his hospitality. The English general would, it was fair to assume, be slaughtered on the spot. Happily it all went wrong. Gordon was as surprised and outraged as

Masupha. As a witness of the occasion wrote to *The Times*:

> Gordon divined his character marvellously, and was the only man Masupha had the slightest regard for. Masupha, if you treat him straightforwardly, is as nice a man as possible, and even kind and thoughtful; but if you treat him the other way, he is a fiend incarnate.

There was nothing feigned about Gordon's indignation, and the chief realized it. Instead of killing him, he regarded him with troubled eyes and asked what he should do. Gordon advised him to have no further dealings with the Cape government until the attack was called off. He then returned to King William's Town and wrote out his resignation. It was, he said, 'impossible to act against natives who I believe are being treated unjustly by the defective government. . . . The Secretary of Native Affairs has admitted certain of these abuses, but it needs more than that admission to satisfy my con- science.' Once again, he had put himself 'into the skin' of those he was with – and, once again, he had come through the experience out of pocket and with no rewards of honour. When, on 14 October, he embarked on the *Kinfauns Castle* for England, he was broke. 'Do you think it is right,' he asked, 'for a major-general in the British Army to set out on a journey like this without sixpence in his pocket?' Perhaps the most rewarding incident in the whole tiresome affair had been a meeting with Cecil Rhodes. The two men had got on splend- idly together; and, afterwards, Rhodes remarked: 'It is curious, but somehow he exercised a strange influence over me.'

Once again, Gordon was unemployed – and, it seemed, un- wanted. Rather than spend a further period in restless idle- ness, he determined to do what he had always wanted to do: visit the Holy Land. Among other things, he wished to map the site of the crucifixion, the Garden of Eden, the boundary between the tribes of Benjamin and Juda, and to pinpoint all the Gideons in which the Bible abounds. He also intended to chart the course of the ark. As somebody said, 'he was not content if he could not give the exact height and breadth of the Deity', and: 'he is a strange mixture of mysticism and measurement.'

He accomplished all that he set out to do, and a good deal more besides. He also contributed much to his store of introspection. On fatalism, for example, he wrote: 'It is a delightful thing to be a fatalist, not as that word is generally employed, but to accept that, when things happen and not before, God has for some strange reason so ordained them to happen – *all* things, not only the great things, but all the circumstances of life.' And: 'We have nothing further to do, when the scroll of events is unrolled, than to accept them as being for the best.' He was happy up to a point – but:

I have now a sense of very great weariness – *not discontent*, but a desire to put off my burden. I believe it is good to be here for myself, else I would not be here, and certainly God gives me comforting thoughts, but one's body is tired of it – and somehow it seems a selfish life, for I see no one for weeks on end.

However, he was not too weary to write a slim volume about his discoveries entitled *Reflections in Palestine*. Unlike all his other work, he actually encouraged its publication. When it appeared, it received a good press from people who knew what they were writing about. When Tourist Gordon combined with Cartographer Gordon and Mystic Gordon, the result, it seemed, was a very competent scholar. He also wrote two thousand pages of letters to his new friend, the Rev Reginald H. Barnes. Gordon was seldom less than articulate – especially when he was on his own.

But 'the scroll of events' was unrolling itself. Prompted by Sir William Mackinnon, chairman of the British India Steam Navigation Company, King Leopold II of Belgium had been anxious to secure Gordon's services for the Congo. It would be a job similar to that which had performed in Equatoria – with the eventual task of taking over from the governor, H. M. Stanley, who was due to retire soon. Gordon had a number of reservations, which mostly centred on the importance of any expedition to the interior being carried out under an international flag. The king had written to him that: 'If you would enter my service, we will examine the question together, and I have no doubt that, with perseverence, we shall solve the problem.' For the moment he had no specific mission to offer him; but, when the time came, Gordon would be able to 'name [his] own terms'. The letter ended with the request that the 'dear General' should believe in his, the king's, 'sincere friendship'.

The time came on 15 October 1883, when a telegram arrived asking Gordon to proceed to the Congo at once. Before he could do so, he had to obtain permission from the War Office. That august body refused, but its reply was misinterpreted by the telegraph clerk at Jaffa. The cable should have read 'declines to sanction': instead, as presented to Gordon, the wording was 'decides to sangdon'. Gordon was happy: the mis-spelling of sanction did not cause him to query the other word. A prolonged spell in the Congo seemed to suggest certain death. Eternity, as he now saw it, was a 'nice house, with garden and no worries'. Now, at last, there seemed to be a short cut. He sailed from Jaffa in a sailing vessel bound for Port Said. On New Year's Day 1884, he presented himself at the king's palace in Brussels. The upshot was that he agreed to go to the Congo in the following month as second-in-command to Stanley, who would retire in the spring. He then hastened back to London, where he commissioned his brother Henry to make his will and put his affairs in order.

The former task was a complicated business. After Gordon's death, it was found that his estate amounted to only just over £2,000. There were, on the other hand, a great many beneficiaries. Most of his twenty-eight nephews and nieces were to receive something, and he wished to be sure that Augusta should never want for a horse and carriage. A few less deserving cases in the tribe of relatives had to be weeded out, and he did this with his sister's help. When the final list was prepared, they both judged it to be very fair.

Meanwhile, he had discovered the telegraph clerk's mistake. The War Office, it seemed, would neither employ him sensibly, nor allow anyone else to secure his services. There was only one thing to do: he would resign his commission. He wrote his letter of resignation on 7 January 1884, and posted it at eleven o'clock that night in a pillar box on the corner of Rockstone Place, Southampton. The War Office never replied.

12
The Expected Guide

When a sick and disillusioned Gordon returned to England from the Sudan at the end of 1879, did he ever pause to consider that he had left his task unfinished – and that, by its incompleteness, he might have done more harm than good? He had taken the cleansing qualities of reform just so far, and then he had quit. *The Times* had said that the job would take much longer, and *The Times* had been right. He had shown the people an intoxicating glimpse of integrity and humanity, and then he had deserted them. Once he had gone, the corrupt Egyptian and Turkish officials, the pashas whose cupidity was only matched by their idleness, and all the parasites which lived off the blood of the enslaved blacks, had swarmed back. But, having tasted justice for however briefly, the victims were unsettled. The affairs of the Sudan could never be quite the same again. For want of Gordon, their minds were wide open to anybody who could offer them an acceptable alternative to the decadent rule of Egypt or, more locally, the villainy of the bashi-bazouks. Turks, Egyptians, Circassians: every one of them was anathema to the natives of the Sudan, and small wonder. But it had needed Gordon to show them just how bad these people were.

Among those who were aware of this situation was a young man named Mohammed Ahmed who had, or so he and his family thought, been touched by the light of the prophet. He was supposed to have received a message that he was the twelfth Imam – the Mahdi, ('the Expected Guide'). There were, of course, signs by which the new prophet could be recognized. He had to be in direct line of descent from

Mohammed: there was no problem on that score. He had to be able to perform miracles. There were enough people to make such claims on his behalf – including his future lieutenant, who avowed that he had been cured of dysentery simply by receiving a smile and a word or two of comfort. His presence had to be 'overflowing with sanctity', which is difficult to define, and must be a matter of opinion, but there was no doubt of his religious zeal and his almost supernatural personality. There was just one small objection, and that was that the Twelfth Imam was expected to come from Jebel Masa in North Africa. However, that was easily overcome. He took the village of Jebel Gedir, which was rather nearer home, and renamed it Jebel Masa. That, in all fairness, was the only flaw in the argument which he used, in May 1881, to proclaim himself the saviour of the Sudan and beyond.

From the sandy cave in which he lived the ascetic life suitable to his 'calling', the self-appointed Mahdi regarded the plight of the Sudanese people. He noticed that taxation was out of all proportion to the amount of property a man owned. He saw that all the positions of minor importance were given to the relatives and friends of those occupying posts of major importance. He no doubt also realized the extent of the slave trade, but this was less important to him. Slavery was a recognized part of the Moslem faith.

When he toured the southern Sudan in search of followers, his realization of the people's plight became more acute. He saw a vast hunger for somebody who could give them hope and inspiration. Like almost every other dictator in history, he did not find power in a vacuum: it grew out of a desperate need. On the one hand, he brought comfort – on the other, a strict code of ethics and a strong reaction against materialism. His demands on his followers were absolute, but he seldom made them in vain.

Truly, the Mahdi was a remarkable man. He *captivated* people. As one of his followers wrote:

On seeing him, I entirely forgot all the troubles I had

suffered on my journey, and was content simply to look at him and listen to his teaching. For several hours, I was too timid to dare to speak to him; but at length I plucked up courage, and in a few words told him my story. . . . I begged him, for the sake of God and his Prophet, to allow me to become one of his disciples. He did so, and gave me his hand, which I kissed most fervently, and I swore entire submission to him as long as I lived.

Although his manner was one of quiet dignity, and even though some people claimed that he was the second coming of Christ, his attitude to his enemies was one of almost fiendish cruelty. He caused those whom he considered to be unbelievers to be murdered, and he encouraged the brutish tradition of decapitating his victims. In Khartoum, his growing influence was viewed with curiosity and then with alarm. But, in Khartoum, there was no leadership worth the name. Raouf Pasha, whom Gordon had sacked, had been appointed governor-general of the Sudan on the 10 January 1880 – a mere month after Gordon's departure. Abu Saoud, whom Gordon had dismissed in Equatoria, had squirmed his way back into a position of relative importance. As Major F. R. Wingate, assistant adjutant-general for intelligence in the Egyptian army, wrote in *Mahdiism and the Egyptian Sudan*, '[Gordon] set the house on fire, and Raouf and Abd el Kader pashas, who succeeded him, could do nothing but watch the flames.'

Despite two abortive attempts by the Khartoum authorities to subdue the Mahdi, his revolution prospered. Conquest was followed by conquest: massacre by massacre. Detached military outposts, tax collectors and government officials were all fair game. Towns and provinces fell, and the authorities in Khartoum became more and more anxious. By 1883, the Mahdi had occupied the whole of Kordofan, and had moved his headquarters to the capital at El Obeid, which had fallen after a siege of five months – during which the greater part of the garrison had died of starvation. El Obeid was about two hundred miles from Khartoum in a south-westerly direction. The governor-general looked anxiously to the north. Egypt would have to send him reinforcements.

Egypt, as it happened, had been having problems of her own. In 1882, one of that country's officers, a fervent nationalist named Arabi Pasha, had decided that the time had come to overthrow the Khedive – and, with him, to topple the European influence on the country. A large part of the army sided with him. The rebels occupied the forts at Alexandria, and the Khedive appealed to the British government for help. It came promptly. Naval units bombarded the forts: on land, a force led by Sir Garnet Wolseley faced up to Arabi's men at Tel-el-Kebir. The battle was brief. When the smoke had blown away, about five thousand Egyptian troops found themselves in chains. As the result of the conflict, Britain, alone of all the European powers, had assumed the role of protector to Egypt. Nevertheless, W. E. Gladstone, the prime minister, made it plain that his country was not concerned with Egypt's domestic policy, and he certainly did not consider that the duties of guardian extended to the Sudan.

Mr Gladstone was emphatic on this point, but when the Khedive asked a retired British officer, Colonel William Hicks, to lead an expeditionary force to Khartoum for the purpose of overthrowing the Mahdi, he had no objection.

The five thousand survivors of Tel-el-Kebir, plus nine European officers, were the nucleus of Hicks's force when it left Cairo. The other ranks departed, according to witnesses, in chains and in tears. The poor fellows had suffered enough. When they reached Omdurman on the opposite bank of the White Nile to Khartoum, they were joined by a large contingent of Sudanese – with this grossly imperfect force, the Colonel proposed to recapture El Obeid. A force of six thousand, which had been promised by the authorities in Equatoria, never arrived.

Hicks built a camp at Omdurman and set about training his ungainly mixture of regular and irregular troops. As Gessi's experience against Suleiman had shown, few of the local men were to be trusted. In that operation, those who were fighting with Gessi on one day might have transferred their allegiance to the slave trader on the next. It all depended on who was winning. As for the Egyptians, they had precious little spirit left in them. A lot of preparation would be needed, Hicks decided, before these men would be a worthy adversary for the Mahdi's army of fanatics.

All this took time, and gave the Mahdi plenty of opportunity to make his own arrangements. He himself was no soldier; he preferred to play the role of the evangelist. The military side of his operations was in the hands of a villainous character named Abdullah el Taasi, who abounded in self-confidence, and was extremely competent. The initial action of the Mahdi and his military leader was brilliant: they dispatched a slave trader named Osman Digna to the eastern Sudan to ferment rebellion. Unless Hicks was very careful, he would find himself fighting on two fronts. To ensure the confidence of his own men, the Mahdi announced that they would be supported in battle by twenty thousand angels specially recruited for the task. When the Prophet made a somewhat far-fetched statement such as this, you did not raise your eyebrows in a cynical grimace; you believed him. It was as much as your life was worth to do otherwise, but this awareness of the price of scepticism was seldom necessary. His personality was so immense and so credible that people really did believe him.

Were there agents of the Mahdi in Hicks's camp? He was certainly badly advised – or else deliberately misled – for how otherwise did this capable officer make such a disastrous mistake when planning his route to El Obeid? Had he travelled a few miles farther to the north, he would have been well supplied with water. As it was, he marched his men through arid desert, where a parching thirst was soon added to all their other miseries. Furthermore, the Mahdi had obviously been told of the proposed offensive, for the column was harried by sharpshooters almost from the moment it set out. Had he concentrated on achieving speed and manoeuvrability, Hicks might have outwitted these skirmishers; but, to his other errors, he had added a burden which gave his force the agility of a slow-witted elephant. Trailing along with the troops, and often getting in their way, were innumerable women – plus no fewer than five thousand camels.

The final battle, if it merits the name, took place at Casghé, which is situated in a wood about thirty-six miles from El Obeid, on either 2, 3 or 4 November (nobody is precisely sure which) 1883. The European officers and a detachment of Turkish cavalry made a desperate stand under the branches of an Adansonia tree. It was of no avail: the entire force was annihilated with the single exception of a former German NCO named Gustav Klootz, who was employed by the *Daily News* correspondent. Klootz had seen the way things were going, and decided to desert. Since he had no very profound views on religion, he found it easy enough to accept the Mahdi's terms that he should adopt the Moslem faith. His life was spared.

The victory increased the Mahdi's prestige even more. He had said that he was invincible, and now it seemed that he really was. By the end of February 1884, Osman Digna had conquered the eastern Sudan, and the rebellion had the entire country in its thrall – from the Equator to the Red Sea, and including Darfur in the west. Egyptian rule now only encompassed Khartoum and the valley of the Nile to the north. It seemed inconceivable that this solitary enclave should not fall before very long.

All this had been taking place when Gordon had been frittering his time in Mauritius and the Cape Colony, and during his exploration of the Holy Land. Now, he was about to sever his final connection with England by setting out on what seemed to him to be a suicidal mission to the Congo. On 9 January 1884, he was down at his sister's house in Southampton, making his preparations for departure, when the door bell was rung by an impressive gentleman with a thick beard, who introduced himself as W. T. Stead, editor of the *Pall Mall*

Gazette. Stead afterwards recalled the first encounter. Gordon was, he wrote,

> a little man and slight of build, with merry blue eyes and curly sandy hair, so simple and unassuming that I took him for a man-servant when he opened the door at his sister's house and helped me off with my overcoat. A man of profound piety, passing much of his time in prayer, he was also a fellow of infinite jest and of the merriest humour. No more delightful companion I ever had. His moods changed like the sky of an April day. Wrath as of the Berserker would flame up, to be succeeded by the humble, self-accusing penitence of a man who feared greatly lest he should have been unjust to his fellow man. No one was more scornful or satirical when speaking of shams and windbags in high places, but his whole face would glow with emotion as he spoke of his 'kings', the ragged urchins whom he had taught at night school.

When Stead had originally requested him for an interview on the Sudan problem, Gordon had asked to be excused. His views, he said, were not important enough to warrant a journey to Southampton. Nevertheless, Stead had decided to make the trip, and he was not to be disappointed. Once the ice had been broken, Gordon showed a great deal of animation, and eventually spoke for two hours on the subject, which he had obviously been following very closely. There were, he said, two alternatives: either total surrender to the Mahdi, or else to hold Khartoum at all costs. 'The Mahdi's forces will fall to pieces of themselves,' he said. 'The garrisons can hold their own at present. Let them continue to hold on until disunion and terrible jealousies have worked their natural results in the camp of the Mahdi.'

He pointed out that, in his opinion, a triumph by the Mahdi would be the cue for dissension by countless self-appointed lesser prophets: 'In all the cities of Egypt it will be felt that what the Mahdi has done they may do; and, as he has driven out the intruder and infidel, they may do the same.' Nor would the spirit of revolt be confined to Egypt. 'Placards have been posted in Damascus calling the population to rise and drive out the Turks. If the whole of the Eastern Sudan is surrendered to the Mahdi, the Arab tribes on both sides of the Red Sea will take fire.'

To withdraw from Khartoum was, in any case, impossible. There were still garrisons holding out in parts of Darfur, Bahr el Ghazal, and Gondokoro. Were they to be abandoned to their fates? What was more, how would the six thousand soldiers at the Sudanese capital be transported north? 'Where are you going to get the camels to take them away?' Gordon asked. 'Will the Mahdi supply them? If they are to escape with their lives, the garrison will not be allowed to leave with a coat on their backs.' What, then, was the answer? The only man fit for power in Egyptian politics was Nubar Pasha. He should be supported 'through thick and thin', and given a free hand. As for the Sudan itself, Gordon made the surprising suggestion that his predecessor as governor of Equatoria, Sir Samuel Baker, should be appointed governor-general – with his brother, Valentine Baker Pasha, in charge of the military. Sir Samuel, he explained, 'possesses the essential energy and single tongue requisite for the office'.

Mr Stead, apparently, thought otherwise. When his newspaper published a long account of the interview on the following day, he made no bones about that fact that he believed Gordon was the man for Khartoum. The *Morning Advertiser* took up the cry, by telling its readers that 'All England has been looking for the employment of General Gordon in the present crisis.' *The Times* continued to write about his impending departure for the Congo, though it hastened to say that Gordon's views were 'entitled to the highest consideration'. It may seem surprising that so much consternation was caused by the rebellious antics of a religious fanatic in a remote and sun-scorched land thousands of miles away. The average Englishman may have been indifferent to the question of who held power in the Sudan; but, once Gordon's name was mentioned, the whole affair seemed to become much more mmediate. It was almost as if the Mahdi was about to occupy Newcastle-upon-Tyne, and that Gordon, much after the manner of Superman, was hurrying to its defence. One might have imagined that the nation, having found a hero, was now desperately anxious to find a situation in which he could perform. The Sudan would do as well as anywhere else.

The government, on the other hand, was less certain of Gordon's suitability to resume his rule over a now broken Sudan; but, then, the government was not very certain about anything in this very difficult situation. Reading from south to north, the commanding officer of such troops as there were in Khartoum was a colonel of French origin named de Coetlogon. He had been one of Hicks's officers, who had been kept back at base to look after the depot. His troops were mostly left-overs from the Hicks force who, for one reason or another, had been fortunate enough to escape the march of death. De Coetlogon did not trust the soldiers, and they had not a great deal of faith in him. He was anxious to get away from this unsavoury place, and, so far as anyone could see, the sooner he went, the better. The current incumbent in what was now a line of failed governor-generals following Gordon's exit, was a gentleman named Abd el Kader, who showed no signs of being any more talented than his predecessors.

Up in Cairo, Tewfik was just hanging on as Khedive by the skin of his teeth. Following the squashing of Arabi Pasha's revolt, the rest of the pashas had scrambled back into power again, with their big brown eyes focused happily on their account books. Evelyn Baring, the former British representative on the Commission of Debts, was carrying out the role of consul-general with, it must be admitted, a good deal to worry him. When 1884 stormed on to the calendar, the skin of Tewfik's teeth gave way at last, and he was deposed. True to Gordon's suggestion (though not because of it) Nubar Pasha set about forming a cabinet on 8 January. Among the people that he dismissed was the foreign minister, Sherif Pasha, who, in the words of *The Times*'s man on the spot, was 'never ambitious, always indolent, thoroughly sceptical as to English notions'. Nubar himself told the correspondent that 'yes; the slave trade may increase in one sense. But it has never ceased. I doubt whether, with our best endeavours, we have lessened the evil in the Sudan in all these years.' Considering the kind words which Gordon was saying about him to Stead on that very day, another of his remarks may have seemed to be lacking in charity. Slavery, he said, had been caused by the very act of trying to suppress it. He spoke of 'conscripts [who] are dragged from their beds to meet their deaths as soldiers in the Sudan'. It was a somewhat harsh reference to Gordon's habit of buying slaves and enlisting them in the army. Since, in theory at any rate, they were paid, they had been given a kind of freedom (though many would no doubt have preferred the unpaid but secure servitude).

Asked whether he proposed to hold Khartoum, Nubar said that this might not be possible. 'I cannot,' he went on, 'have on my shoulders the responsibility for 6,000 lives because of a question of my *amour propre*' – all of which sounded quite good, though it would be interesting to know to what extent this statement had been inspired by the British government, via Baring, which was known to be against any attempt to hold the Sudanese capital. It was a view which, certainly, ran counter to French opinion, as expressed in that country's newspaper, *Temps*. If Khartoum were to be abandoned, it told its readers, the result would be to destroy the achievements of twenty-five years of labour

> which have been directed towards implanting civilization in Central Africa. Negro barbarianism will force back civilization, and the slave trade, the plague of the African Continent . . . will again devour those flourishing countries from which Englishmen have succeeded in extirpating it.

And so to London, where a Liberal government was headed by W. E. Gladstone, who was much concerned with a new Reform Bill, and a great deal less than enthusiastic about the Sudan. Indeed, it sometimes seemed that the prime minister hoped that, if he closed his eyes for long enough, the whole wretched problem of Khartoum, the Sudan, and the supposedly sovereign states of Egypt, would go away and never return. His minister of war and leader of the party was Lord Hartington, a blue-blooded statesman who was once heard to mutter that 'the proudest moment in his life' had been when his pig won the prize at Skipton Fair. The foreign secretary, Lord Granville, came from scarcely less noble stock. He was a plodder, if that counts for anything, but that was about all. One looked in vain for him to produce the apt word, the deft stroke of diplomacy, or the inspired solution to any problem – no matter how humble it might be.

Summarized, the events to which this trio had applied its attention with varying degrees of concern looks something like this:

23 November 1883: Baring reports to Granville that the Egyptian government is determined to hold the Sudan.

24 November 1883: News of the Hicks disaster at last filters through. Egypt decides that it is impossible to hold Khartoum, and the seat of Sudanese government will have to be moved to Berber.

25 November 1883: Granville informs Baring that the British government can do nothing to help. He is to instruct the Egyptian government to 'keep on the defensive' (whatever that might mean).

Baring telegraphs to Granville that the Egyptians would be unable to hold the Sudan without help. They would have to withdraw their garrisons to Egypt.

Col de Coetlogon informs Baring that Khartoum will fall in two months' time. He recommends withdrawal to Berber, from which an escape route could be opened up to the coast at Suakim.

3 December 1883: Baring reports to Granville a proposal to send the arch-slave-trader, Zebehr Pasha, to Suakim. From the wings, as it were, Gordon comments that Zebehr will be taken prisoner by the Mahdi, but will end up leading the revolt.

Lord Granville makes it clear that he will not send British or Indian troops to the Sudan.

13 December 1883: Granville announces that he has no objection to Turkish troops being used – provided the Turkish government pays them, and they are restricted to operations in the Sudan.

21 December 1883: Sherif Pasha objects to the advice of the British government. Egypt cannot abandon territorities (i.e. the Sudan) which are necessary for the country's security. This is no doubt a reaction to an observation by Baring that the country to the north of Wadi Halfa and the Red Sea ports is as much as 'Egypt can govern with advantage to itself'.

22 December 1883: Baring agrees that, to abandon territory, would be a serious blow to the Khedive's authority, and might cause friendly tribes and Bedouins to turn against the government. But – Baring tells Granville that 'It would be necessary to send an English officer of high authority to Khartoum with full powers to withdraw the garrison and make the best arrangements for the future government of the country.'

This is the first intimation that anybody is thinking of sending a man of Gordon's calibre to the Sudan. Once the article on the front page of the *Pall Mall Gazette* had stirred up popular opinion at home, Gordon's name appeared more and more frequently in the telegrams which passed between Baring and Granville. The original suggestion came from Granville, but Baring cabled back that such a solution would not be acceptable to the Egyptians (did Nubar have unpleasant memories of the day Gordon challenged him to a duel?). Eventually, the foreign secretary felt bound to send a telegram to Mr Gladstone, who was out of town. 'If,' he wrote, 'Gordon says he believes he could, by his personal influence, excite the tribes to escort the Khartoum garrison and its inhabitants to Suakim, a little pressure on Baring might be advisable.' Mr Gladstone agreed. Neither statesman seemed to be aware that Gordon had said nothing of the kind – and was unlikely to.

As for the popular hero, he was still planning to take up his appointment in the Congo. He made a brief trip down to

Heavitree near Exeter, where he spent the night at the vicarage of his friend, the Rev R. H. Barnes. During the visit, he and the clergyman drove over to a neighbouring village to call on Sir Samuel Baker.

While we were driving from Newton Abbot to Sandford Orleigh [Barnes recalled] Sir Samuel Baker pressed on Gordon the expedience of his again going to the Sudan as Governor-General, if Her Majesty's Government should require it. Gordon was silent, but his eyes flashed, and an eager expression passed over his face as he looked at his host. Late at night, when we had retired, he came to my room, and said in a soft voice, 'You saw me today?' 'You mean in the carriage?' 'Yes; you saw *me* – that was *myself* – the self I want to get rid of.'

He went back to Southampton to pack. He was due to leave for Brussels on 16 January. On the 15th, however, he was summoned to the War Office by his old friend, Garnet Wolseley. Would he, Wolseley wanted to know, have any objection to going back to the Sudan? Gordon said that he would not – although there was the question of his engagement by King Leopold of Belgium. The two men seem to have left it at that. Gordon departed for Brussels. But, on the following day, a crucial telegram was received at the Foreign Office from Baring.

Gordon [the consul-general had written] would be the best man if he would pledge himself to carry out the policy of withdrawing from the Sudan as quickly as is possible consistently with saving life. He must also understand that he must take his instructions from the British representative in Egypt.... I would rather have him than anyone else, provided there is a perfectly clear understanding with him as to what his position is to be and what line of policy he is to carry out. Otherwise not ...

No sooner had Gordon arrived in Brussels than, to the annoyance of the Belgian king, he was summoned back to

London. He was presented to a meeting of the Cabinet ministers and agreed to travel out to Suakim and report on the situation. There was no talk of assuming responsibility for the evacuation of Khartoum, and certainly none of holding the place. He was simply to visit the country as an observer. It was, they congratulated themselves, an honourable gesture – and cheaper than sending a military expedition.

Eight weeks had passed since the question of sending him to the Sudan first arose. It took him eight hours to prepare to go there. On the night of 18 January, he was once again at Victoria Station – this time in the company of an officer in the Hussars named Colonel J. D. H. Stewart, who was to become his second-in-command. Stewart had been on duty in the Sudan in the previous year, and his knowledge of the country was said to be second only to Gordon's. As a mark of respect – a final gesture, one might say, by the government – Wolseley and the Duke of Cambridge were on the platform to see him off, and Lord Granville bought the tickets. Charles Gordon's last action on British soil was to commission Wolseley to purchase a number of copies of Dr Samuel Clarke's *Scripture Promises*. He was to have one delivered to each member of the Cabinet on the following morning. When the news of his departure was published next day, *The Times* described it as 'a welcome surprise to the country'. But, by then, Gordon and Stewart were well on their way towards Brindisi, from whence they were due to travel to Port Said. Gordon's last great adventure had begun.

13
The Road Back to Khartoum

In the train to Brindisi, and on the ship which took him to the eastern end of the Mediterranean, Gordon had been thinking about his coming mission. One man occupied most of his thoughts: the notorious slave trader and father of Suleiman, Zebehr. Gordon had been Zebehr's undoing. He had been responsible for the death of his son: if he had been backed up by the Egyptian authorities, he would have caused the slaver's execution as well. In 1879, he had signed Zebehr's death warrant, and had him sent off to Cairo under armed guard. In the Egyptian capital, however, the sentence had been commuted. Since then, the man had been released from prison and was living under surveillance. He was, as most people realized, politically dangerous. Amid all the weak and slothful, mercenary and indecisive, characters who contributed their output of hot air to the salons of Cairo, Zebehr stood out. He was firm and strong, and totally ruthless in indulging his taste for power.

At first, Gordon considered that this human powder keg was too dangerous to remain on Egyptian territory. The Mahdi on his own was effective enough: if, by whatever way, he became allied with Zebehr, the results would confound the imagination. Gordon took a telegraph form, and wrote a message to Evelyn Baring. Zebehr should, in his opinion, be banished to Cyprus. But then Gordon thought again. Guided by what he described as a 'mystic feeling', he decided that he had been wrong about the slave trader. Far from having potential to assist the undoing of the Sudan, he might actually be the very man to save it.

His reasoning was simple. His present task might be concerned with the evacuation of the country, but that was only part of the problem. If Khartoum were abandoned without leaving behind a strong governor-general, the Mahdi would march in and his success would be absolute. As the past few years had made painfully clear, there was nobody fit to undertake the office except – and Gordon's 'mystic feeling' must have faltered for a moment before he pronounced the name – Zebehr. In his feverish, and often unrealistic, optimism, he saw no reason why past feuds could not be forgotten. The British major-general and the Arab slave trader could, he felt sure, work peaceably and constructively together.

Whether Zebehr would take a similar view was doubtful. In a letter to his son, he had condemned Gordon for threatening

> all that we have accomplished by our unstinted personal exertion, and by the expenditure of large sums in the conquest of countries, leading to the security of the inhabitants (God's servants, or subjects of the Government), and to the enlargement and extension of the beneficient sway of the very great Khedive, with purity of intent and perfect devotion

and so on and so forth. He was not the first businessman to suffer delusions of philanthropic grandeur, and he would certainly not be the last.

In England – where citizens lived starry-eyed beneath a Liberal government, secure in their faith in reform and in the power of good to free the oppressed – the proposed appointment would be seen as a disaster for humanity. The Mahdi was not necessarily evil: not by any manner of means. He was leading a subject people out of the wilderness, and who cared how much blood he shed in the process? The situation was dangerous: no doubt about that. It threatened the ports on the Red Sea and, ultimately, the passage of British ships to India by way of Suez. But – to put a villain of Zebehr's calibre in control of the Sudan's government – the idea was unthinkable! Gordon was on his way there, and that

198

was all that mattered. A meeting of minds between the prototype hero and the prototype villain, Zebehr, was unthinkable.

Nevertheless, at some point during his short stay in Cairo, where he broke his journey to Suakim, a meeting was arranged between Gordon and Zebehr. Whatever 'mystic feelings' the former may have experienced certainly did not extend to 'the greatest slave hunter who ever existed'.* The encounter began badly, with Zebehr refusing to shake Gordon's hand, and it seems to have degenerated into a swearing match. Colonel Watson, who was present, afterwards observed that, to send Zebehr to Khartoum, would certainly be the death of one of them – probably of both. Baring came to a similar conclusion and put it on record that the slaver was far too hostile ever to work with Gordon.

Looking back on it, this brief period in Cairo radically changed the nature of Gordon's assignment. As instructed by the cabinet ministers, he was going to the Sudan only as an observer. His job was to study the situation, write a report and make recommendations, and then to come home as quickly as possible. But the Khedive, apparently, had other ideas. He appointed Gordon governor-general of the Sudan – albeit without pay. This changed matters completely. He now had an executive role to perform, and the question of his responsibility had to be looked at again. Was he still, as the cabinet had insisted, to come under Evelyn Baring's orders, or was his duty now to the Khedive of Egypt? Had Gordon stuck to his original plan, and gone straight to Suakim, he would probably have been back in England within a month or two. Who knows – he might even have survived to become an eccentric retired general spinning out the evening of his life in Tunbridge Wells.

Gordon's departure from Cairo verged on the burlesque. He, himself, was suitably attired for his mission by wearing a fez.

---

* Gordon's description of him. A more favourable portrait from a newspaperman referred to him as 'a quiet, far-seeing, thoughtful man of iron will – a born ruler of men'.

As many people said, it suited him. Also on the train complete with his twenty-three wives, was the Emir Abdul Shakur, who had been dug out of retirement and given the unenviable task of occupying Darfur. The Emir was as unhappy about his appointment as Gordon was about his fitness for it. After days of bickering aboard the steamer, during which the Egyptian tried to soothe his misery by heavy drinking, the wretched man finally disembarked at Dongola and returned with his wives to Cairo. One doubts whether Darfur was the the poorer for his flight.

Gordon continued what turned out to be a triumphal progress. At every point on his journey to Khartoum, he was hailed as a kind of saviour. At some point on the trip, he must have passed de Coetlogon, who had left Khartoum at about the time Gordon had departed from Cairo. Back at the British residency, Gordon had said that he would take eighteen days to complete the journey: in fact, it took twenty. When he arrived in the city at nine thirty on the morning of 18 February, the population went wild with relief and excitement. As Frank Power, *The Times* correspondent who was also carrying out the role of British consul, observed: 'The fellows in Lucknow did not look more anxiously for Colin Campbell than we are looking for Gordon.' The man, who was supposed to offer deliverance from the Mahdi's threat, came without troops or money, but that did not seem to matter when Gordon's magic was present. As the newly re-appointed governor-general told people, 'I will not fight with any weapons but justice.' He also wrote to Augusta that 'I hope, D.V., to get all settled in a few weeks.' Did he really believe either statement? He was undoubtedly given to moments of frenetic optimism, but such wild claims were beyond reason. At all events, he made his attitude to the rights of the individual clear at once. His first action on moving into the Palace was to order the tax records to be burned; to release all the prisoners from the city's gaol; and to have the stocks, the whips, and the branding irons destroyed in the public square. It was the old Gordon, whom they knew and loved, restored to them; but with one difference. He was not compelled to admit that he accepted slavery. As he said, he was powerless to prevent it. Once he was gone, it would return in any case, and one might as well admit the fact. But was this, also, a peace feeler directed at Zebehr? In spite of their unfortunate meeting in Cairo, he still believed that this man was the solution to the present crisis, and that nothing much could be achieved without him.

Khartoum was like an island connected to the world of security and (some people would have said) sanity, by the thin and tenuous ribbon of the Nile. All the country around it was occupied by the Mahdi and his ever-growing army of Dervishes. Within the capital there were three Englishmen – Gordon, Stewart, and Power – plus a handful of European consuls, and a population of troops and officials and civilians amounting to about forty thousand. Food and ammunition were not yet to become a problem: money, or the lack of it, was. The funds, which were supposed to have been sent from Cairo, never arrived. Nevertheless, the siege of Khartoum did not really begin until 12 March. Until then, Gordon could have considered himself free to work on his own government's intention to evacuate this precariously held stronghold. Whether he ever intended to carry out this idea is another matter.

His position was a strange one. The Khedive had appointed him governor-general with all the responsibility which this illustrious position seems to imply. He did not, however, intend to pay him anything. Gordon's salary remained a matter for the British government, and the ministers had made it perfectly clear that he was to implement their policy (and not the Khedive's, assuming that he had one – which seems unlikely), and that he was responsible to Baring (and not to the Khedive). Gordon was never one to fight shy of the written word. During the first few months of his assignment, telegrams poured up the Eastern Telegraph Company's line to Cairo in an endless procession of dots and dashes. He protested again and again about the refusal to employ Zebehr, but the real bombshell arrived on the British consul-general's desk in mid-April. In it, Gordon reiterated that

> of course my duty is evacuation and the best I can hope for is establishing a quiet government. The first I hope to accomplish. The second is a difficult task and concerns Egypt more than me. If Egypt is to be quiet, *Mahdi must be smashed up* [author's italics]. Mahdi is most unpopular, and with care and time could be smashed. Remember that, once Khartoum belongs to Mahdi, the task will be far more difficult. . .

The words were terrifying. As Sir Charles Dilke, the president of the local government board, said when he heard them: 'Gordon has frightened us out of our senses.' They seemed to confirm the opinion of Lord Rendel, a close friend of Gladstone, who had suggested that long experience of savage lands had made Gordon 'useless for civilized work'. Dilke's own opinion was that he had become 'a wild man under the influence of Central Africa, which acts upon the sanest man like strong drink'.

It was a remarkable coincidence that the two most formidable adversaries to confront the mystical soldier Charles Gordon were both of them religious fanatics. The Heavenly King in China had received his instructions direct from God. The Mahdi was in no doubt about where his own mission originated. In both cases, one cannot help imagining, there might have been a bond of sympathy between the British commander and his by no means heathen foe. In fact, there was none: indeed, Gordon does not seem to have had any great understanding of his opponents' beliefs. The practical soldier, in both instances, elbowed the mystic out of the way. In China, of course, his task had been very much easier. He was fighting an offensive war, with all the advantages of mobility on his side, and with perfectly clear instructions. In Khartoum, the instructions were clear enough, but nobody seems to have spent a great deal of thought on how they should be carried out. At the best, he would have to lead a mixed population

hrough a wilderness of many hundreds of miles of potentially
1ostile territory. At the worst, he would have to contain himself in Khartoum, waiting – for what?

When, over in the east, General Valentine Baker led his
force of four thousand irregulars against Osman Digna, he
was roundly thrashed. Two key towns fell, and it looked as if
the Red Sea port of Suakim would not be long in following.
To protect it, Sir Charles Graham was dispatched from Cairo
with a force of British regulars. In two battles – at El Teb and
Tamai – he inflicted heavy casualties on the rebels, and secured
the port. Would the troops then march inland and provide
sinews for the defence of Khartoum during an evacuation?
The Times suggested that this was likely. The government
entertained no such notions. When, in the House of Lords,
Granville was asked by Lord Strathnairn whether he could
consider postponing the withdrawal of troops from Suakim –
so that they could be sent to the relief of Gordon – the foreign
secretary replied that there were problems concerning the
health of the men and their water supplies. A long march to
the interior would be altogether too much for them. That, at
least, is what he is believed to have said. Lord Granville had
a tiresome habit of muttering. All too often, reports of his
Parliamentary utterances were qualified by the words 'was
understood to reply'.

When Gordon arrived in Khartoum, he did not think it
beyond the bounds of possibility that he might achieve some
sort of understanding with the Mahdi. One of his first actions
was to send the rebel leader a fine suit of clothes as a gift, and
a polite letter on the lines of 'can't we talk things over'. In it,
he offered him the governorship of Kordofan, and requested
the release of prisoners. The Mahdi's reply was derisory. Why,
he wanted to know, should he be offered something which he
had already taken by force of arms? He returned Gordon's
gifts, and sent with them a dirty jacket, an overcoat, cap,
girdle and beads, of the type that his own supporters wore.
They were, he explained, 'the clothing of those who have given
up the world'. The words might have been Gordon's, but

this does not seem to have occurred to him. He kicked them into a corner, and dispatched the following curt note: 'I have received the letters sent by your three messengers, and I understand all their contents; but I cannot have any more communications with you.' It was, to all intents and purposes, a declaration of war.

Gordon's routine was now divided into two parts. On the one hand, there were the long sessions at his desk, scribbling off one telegram after another to Baring: on the other, he was busy preparing defences for the city. When, on 5 May, it seemed to Baring that the evacuation of Khartoum was taking an unreasonably long time, he asked Gordon to state his 'cause and intention in staying in Khartoum, knowing Government means to abandon Sudan'. Gordon's reply was brief and to the point. 'I stay at Khartoum,' he explained, 'because the Arabs have shut us up, and will not let us out . . . no one would leave more willingly than I, if it were possible.' In fact, he had been able to send a number of people north. Among them, were a good many women and children, and he had asked Nubar Pasha to 'send a kind-hearted man to meet them'. Within the city, he took care not to neglect the spiritual welfare of his men. They were ordered to hold regular morning and evening prayers: church parades were compulsory every Friday (the Moslem sabbath), and, over the chair of state in the audience chamber of the palace, there was an Arabic text displayed. 'God rules the hearts of all men,' it announced.

The Sudanese and Egyptian troops had little affection for one another. Consequently, the former were sent across the river to Hicks's old camp at Omdurman. So far as the defences were concerned, the Nile seemed to supply all the protection that was needed on one side: on the others, he ordered three lines of percussion mines to be laid down. There were also crowsfeet, barbed wire entanglements, and even broken glass. The Nile, as it happened, was not to be relied upon. When it was in full spate, it was formidable enough; but, after a long period of drought, it was useless. No doubt, Gordon believed that this shortcoming was unimportant. He had, after all, a

mall navy of eleven river boats which was his most formid-
ble weapon.

Each vessel was about the same size, and built to the same
design, as the old 'penny steamboats' which used to ply the
Thames. In the bows, a small turret, in which a 9-pounder
brass howitzer was mounted, was constructed from baulks of
timber. Between the paddle boxes amidships, there was another turret and another gun. Aft of this, an enclosure made
from cast-iron plate had been built to protect the helmsman
and to provide cover for riflemen. The sides and bulwarks were
also protected with metal plate, and the portion of the boiler
which projected above the deck was covered in a jacket manufactured from logs of wood. It would stop bullets, but not
shells. The crews lived off the countryside. All told, there
were three holds. The forward compartment was crammed
with ammunition. The main holds contained a mixture of
women, stowaways, goats and plunder; and the after hold was
loaded with the captain's possessions. There were rats everywhere, the dirt was indescribable, and the vessels stank. The
crews were a mixture of Egyptians and Sudanese. In one of
them, the overall commander of the ship and the soldiers was
an Egyptian. The officer in charge of the regular soldiers was
a Sudanese; the troops themselves were freed slaves; an
Egyptian was in charge of the artillery; the captain came from
Dongola; and the engineering staff were Egyptians. By some
miracle, it seems to have worked, for these vessels were far
more effective than the land-based troops.

Gordon had received the Mahdi's reply to his peace offering on 10 March. Six days later, he dispatched a force to
engage detachments of Dervishes which were massing at
Halfaya about eight miles downstream. The action was a
disaster. Colonel Stewart was in overall command of about
a thousand men, most of them bashi-bazouks, and one cannon.
The Mahdi's men had taken up a fortified position, and
Stewart's intention was to destroy it 'without too much loss'.
His plan was to divide his force into two. One party was to
storm the position – covered by the cannon and the rifle fire of

the other. The two Egyptian commanders were a pair c officers named Hassan Pasha and Seyid Pasha whose abilit had yet to be put to the test.

The troops landed on the right bank of the Nile without an opposition. The covering force formed up, and the bash bazouks advanced uncertainly towards the objective. As th men approached the stockade, sixty rebel horsemen brok cover and galloped in their direction. The attackers fired on ragged volley, and then fled. Meanwhile, the covering infantr had formed a square. As the Dervish cavalry approache them, they too made off in the direction of the river. Wit their morale completely broken, they plodded back to th boat with their rifles shouldered. The horsemen picked off th stragglers, and the beaten troops refused to open fire. Thre hundred and fifty men were killed or wounded, the canno and a large quantity of ammunition were lost, and the Der vishes sustained no casualties at all.

When Gordon heard about it, he was extremely angry. H came to the conclusion that the only soldiers who could b relied upon were the Sudanese. The Egyptian and Arab troop were useless – even when they were required to fight to sav their own lives. Two hundred and fifty bashi-bazouks were dis missed on the spot, and Hassan and Seyid were shot fo 'treachery'. But Gordon could only be ruthless for a shor time. Behind the iron man, we seem to see the figure of th white rabbit from *Alice in Wonderland*, glancing impatientl at his watch, tut-tutting about wasted time, and then scurryin off on some errand. The British public carved him into a hero a man of resolution, who never for a moment doubted himsel or his cause. The truth was very different. Inside, he was curious mixture of determination and uncertainty, a man i whom there was an almost continuous conflict between militar duty and Christian compassion. Having witnessed the execu tion of the two pashas, he at once began to torture himsel about the rightness of it. In the end, compassion won, but i was too late. All that he could do was to promise to pay th relatives of each £1,000 by way of compensation.

His rage, as always, was fit to make all tremble. He knew this, and it worried him. 'I have led,' he confided in his journal, 'the officers and officials the lives of dogs while I have been up here. It is quite painful to see men tremble so when they come and see me, that they cannot hold a match to their cigarette.' Later, when the Mahdi's men attacked and captured Omdurman, the telegraph boy at the palace failed to wake him up and tell him about the assault. Gordon flew into a rage and boxed the lad's ears. 'And then,' he wrote, 'as my conscience pricked me, I gave him five dollars. He said he did not mind if I killed him – I was his father.'

The northward flow of telegrams to Baring continued. Gordon had now worked out his plan, and, as always, it depended upon Zebehr. The slave trader was to be appointed ruler of the Sudan, for which he was to be paid £6,000 a year by the Egyptian government. He would be free to appoint and discharge officials. Equatoria, Fashoda and Bahr-el-Gazal were to be abandoned, but the Sudan was to be held. British troops would be used to carry on the war against the Dervishes until Khartoum was relieved, but Zebehr was to be personally responsible for the capture of the Mahdi and the release of his prisoners. He was to be paid £30,000 for accomplishing this. As Gordon confided to Frank Power, who was still doubling up as *The Times* correspondent and British consul, 'As for Zebehr Pasha's blood feud with me, it is absurd!' All that was needed to secure his loyalty, he felt sure, was that 'a subsidy be granted him for three years dependent on my safety'. It may seem strange, coming from a man who had once sentenced the slave trader to death, but Gordon now began to defend Zebehr's actions. He was, he suggested, no worse than many another man. 'The thief,' he pointed out, 'is no worse than the receiver.' But nobody paid any attention to his protests. He was not to be given the assistance of his old enemy, and that was that.

The situation was deteriorating rapidly. As Gordon was continually pointing out, the fact that the evacuation of the Sudan had been announced, and that women and children had already been seen passing down the Nile towards the Egyptian frontier at Wadi Halfa, had been of inestimable help to the Mahdi. It made matters seem as if his victory had already been accomplished, and its effect on moral was appalling. The average Sudanese must have frequently asked himself what was to happen, when the operation had been completed. He would be at the Mahdi's mercy, and the many reports of atrocities had shown that it amounted to nothing at all. Might it not be as well to cut one's losses, and go over to him before it was too late?

To the north of Khartoum, tribes which had hitherto held out, now went over to the Mahdi. On 26 May, Berber fell: the escape route to the north was cut and, with it, the telegraph line to Cairo. Gordon's agent in the town, a Swiss gentleman named Giuseppe Cuzzi, managed to save his skin by hastily adopting the Moslem faith. Five thousand other people were less fortunate. They were massacred by the Dervishes in an orgy of bloodshed, which followed a bloodless victory. As an exhibition of religious enlightenment, it left a good deal to be desired, but the Mahdi does not seem to have minded. Cuzzi was no doubt prudent, though Gordon was unable to appreciate his point of view. When, later on, the Mahdi dispatched his Swiss prisoner as an emissary to Khartoum, he refused to see him. To his journal, he confided how much he 'lamented ... the degeneracy of the *Faith*, when Christians became Mussulmans, and Mussulmans became followers of the False Prophet, to save their property.'

Gordon realized that he needed help badly, but where was it to come from? If only two hundred British troops would come to Wadi Halfa; if a force of Indian Moslems could be landed at Suakim and marched to Berber; so little was required to accomplish so much! But the line was dead, and no troops came. In desperation, before the communications had been cut, he had sent a letter to Sir Samuel Baker in England. Could he not appeal to British and American millionaires for £300,000? He should then engage three thousand Turkish troops, and send them to Khartoum. 'This would settle the

Sudan and Mahdi forever,' he wrote. And he added: 'I do not see the fun of being caught here to walk the streets for years as a Dervish, with sandalled feet; not that (D.V.) I will ever be taken alive.' Again: nothing happened.

Already, time seemed to be running out. Shortly before the fall of Berber, Power had informed his editor that 'I do not think we shall send any more cables, for it is no longer a question of days, but of hours.' He was, perhaps, pessimistic – especially as Gordon had just told him:

> I am dead against the sending of any British expedition to reconquer the Sudan. It is unnecessary. I would not have a single life lost . . . I like the people in rebellion as much as those who are not, and I thank God that, so far as I am concerned, no man has gone before his maker prematurely.

This statement was not entirely accurate: there had been that appalling fiasco at Halfayah, and even heavier casualties were soon to follow. But he had a great many other things to think about.

Money was a perpetual problem. Prices were rising by as much as three thousand per cent and the city was, literally, running out of cash. However, Gordon was nothing if not ingenious. For want of anything better, he caused his own currency to be printed. With it, he made up the arrears of pay due to the troops: by the end of July, he had distributed £50,000. There should also, he decided, be some system of rewards. In July, he designed a medal. It was in the shape of a star, with a grenade in the centre, and it came in three classes: gold, silver and pewter. Women and children, just as much as soldiers, were eligible to receive it for acts of self-sacrifice and gallantry.

Once Berber had fallen, the Mahdi's forces began to advance on the city by way of the Blue Nile. Gordon's plan was now to remove this threat by clearing the enemy away from the river as far as Sennar, where a garrison was still presumed to be holding out. When this had been accomplished, Stewart was to be sent down-river to Berber with the object of recapturing the town and opening up the escape route again. The plan never got very far. At the end of August, an officer named Mohammed Pasha set off up the Blue Nile with over one thousand men. On his first day in action, he was successful: he routed the Dervishes and captured sixteen hundred rifles plus a large number of swords and spears. Gordon was delighted. He went out on one of the steamers to congratulate him, and promoted him to the rank of general on the spot. For the next few days, things went equally well, but success was making Mohammed Bey careless. On 5 September, shortly after dawn, he and his men marched into a wood, where they were ambushed. Within a comparatively short space of time, half of his force (including himself) had been wiped out, and the Dervishes were the richer by 980 rifles. After this setback, any attempt to retake Berber was out of the question.

Throughout this period, Colonel Stewart had been keeping a diary of events. Gordon was now anxious that this document should be conveyed to Egypt. The statesmen seemed to care little about the plight of Khartoum: perhaps it would help matters, if he had a chance of putting his case before the world. He had also written a letter to Baring, which he intended should go with it. 'How many times have we written asking for reinforcements?' he demanded. 'No answer at all times has come to us ... and the hearts of men have become weary at this delay. While you are eating and drinking and resting on good beds, we and those with us ... are watching night and day, endeavouring to quell the movement of this false Mahdi.' The mission would be dangerous, and Gordon was in some doubt about whom to entrust it to. Eventually he decided to send Stewart, Power and the French consul, Herbin. With a party of twelve Greeks they set off on 8 September in the steamer *Abbas*, with strict orders to trust nobody on shore.

Not until two months later did Gordon hear the tragic fate of the ship: she ran aground near Abu Hamed, a small town on the edge of the Baiuda Desert, and all her passengers were massacred except the stoker who managed to escape after four months in captivity.

Back in July, Power had written that he expected Khartoum to be able to hold out for two months longer. Every day, as he stood at his favourite vantage point of the roof of the palace, searching the horizon with his telescope, Gordon must have hoped to see some signs of a column of reinforcements approaching. There were none. There were, on the other hand a host of rumours, most of which confidently asserted that an English force would be arriving on the following day. There was even one which stated that 'the Queen of England has arrived at Dongola'. On further consideration, it was decided that this must refer to the name of a steamer.

The Mahdi's forces were closing in on the city. The casualties inflicted on the defending force were very moderate, and Gordon had no way of calculating the number of Dervishes killed. Early on in the siege, he had forbidden his men to decapitate the enemy's dead. It may have been customary, but it was unpleasant. The fact that it might enable him to count heads was a poor excuse. As for the troops themselves, Gordon had long ago realized that the Sudanese were the only ones to be relied upon. As he said, 'one Arab horseman is enough to put two hundred of the bulk of our men to flight.' To encourage recruitment, he sent agents out into the countryside, offering freedom to any slave who enlisted. The response was not very great.

He was now the only Englishman in the place – alone and, one suspects, often lonely. Back in Britain, however, he was far from forgotten. The news which reached London was scanty and only very occasional. Ironically, the most reliable courier from the beleagured city was one of Zebehr's men. Such information as he managed to get through was enough to convince people that Gordon was, as they had always believed, the very stuff of heroes. A leader writer on *The Times* stated

No Englishman can read [about Gordon's plight] without a thrill of pride and a flush of shame. In the long roll of Englishmen who have spent themselves in the service of

England, there is no brighter name than that won for himself by General Gordon, nor in the glorious catalogue of their exploits is there any that can outshine the defence of Khartoum.

It was powerful stuff. Unfortunately, the only person who seemed to be unmoved by it was Mr Gladstone – although, as that politician might have pointed out, Gordon was not really 'spending himself' in the service of England. He had taken up the cause of a country which, as the newspaper had suggested several weeks earlier, could only restore itself to a state of 'tranquillity and contentment'. 'by rigorous and upright administration'. Tranquillity and contentment! The only people who enjoyed such comforts were the British residents and the over-fed pashas in Cairo. As for Mr Gladstone, he knew that the Turks were never far away from Egyptian politics, and his views on them were uncompromising. Back in 1877, he had told the House of Commons that they, 'one and all, bag and baggage, shall, I hope, clear out from the province they have desolated and profaned.' No wonder Gordon's appeal for Turkish reinforcements had gone unheeded.

14
The Reluctant Rescue Operation

Throughout the siege of Khartoum, William Ewart Gladstone was seen to show emotion on only one occasion. It happened, ironically enough, on the day that Colonel Stewart and his companions were massacred. He was up in Aberdeen at the time, attending some Liberal party function, when he chanced to look at the local newspaper. The bulk of its contents was devoted to an over-enthusiastic account of his welcome in the city, but he happened to notice a short item of news from Khartoum, tucked away among the acres of printed applause. After four months' silence, it seemed, a dispatch had been received from Gordon. It told of his plan (long abandoned) for sending a raiding party by steamer to Berber. This, coupled with memories of Gordon's earlier talk of 'smashing up the Mahdi', enraged the prime minister. As he read on, according to one of his companions, 'his face hardened and whitened, the eyes burned as I have seen them once or twice in the House of Commons – burned with a deep fire as if they would have consumed the paper on which Gordon's message was printed.' There was no doubt in Gladstone's mind: if the Mahdi had belonged to a British political party, he would, with his radical views, have been a Liberal. With 'a brow like thunder', he stalked out of the room, and was not seen again that night. By the following morning, he had exorcized his rage by writing an order for Gordon to be relieved of his governor-generalship of the Sudan. He was now to be simply governor of Khartoum and its immediate surroundings.

Normally, Mr Gladstone was less decisive about matters relating to Gordon. He would fob questions off with such

213

evasive answers as 'there is nothing to show he is in danger'; and, when all else failed, he would simply refuse to say anything at all. In any case, he knew very little about the Sudan. For most of the time, he was far more concerned about his own health, and with a new Reform Bill that he was trying to push through Parliament. When it was suggested that a relief force might be dispatched to Khartoum, he retorted that: 'I do not consider the evidence as to Gordon's position justifies, in itself, military preparations for the contingency of a military expedition.' On other occasions, he would insist that every member of the cabinet should be consulted – knowing that they were all out of London. Lord Granville, his toady, was no better. In his opinion, 'when a number of men volunteer for a forlorn hope ... there is no obligation in honour on the commander of the army to risk any more lives in saving that forlorn hope.' Perhaps, his indistinct speech in the House of Commons really did not matter. He seldom said anything worth listening to.

On 1 April, Power had written for *The Times* that 'we cannot bring ourselves to believe that we are to be abandoned by the Government.' It might have been better if the government in question had paid more attention to his reports, which conveyed an accurate and vivid impression of the situation in Khartoum. As it was, they did not seem to be capable of appreciating how isolated the city was – and, when a period of four months went by without any word from Gordon, it never occurred to them that he might not be able to communicate. He was, they concluded, in a huff. It was the kind of conduct one might expect from a man who had already shown himself to be a considerable eccentric.

Even Baring, who was a careful career man and not inclined to take any action which might displease his superiors, became worried by the Gladstonian indifference. In one telegram, he pleaded: 'Let me earnestly beg Her Majesty's Government to place themselves in the position of Gordon.' It is doubtful whether Mr Gladstone cared to do anything of the kind. In any case, he was out of town – convalescing from one of his illnesses. Fortunately, there were others who were more concerned with the plight of this lonely Englishman. Queen Victoria telegraphed Lord Hartington that 'Gordon is in danger. You are bound to try and save him. Surely Indian Troops might go from Aden. They could bear the climate. You have incurred fearful responsibility.' Later on, she told Gladstone that he must take some action – 'if not for humanity's sake, for the honour of the Government and nation, Gordon must not be abandoned.'

At a lower level, Gordon's old friend, General Wolseley said: 'I don't wish to share the responsibility of leaving Charlie Gordon to his fate, and it is for this reason that I recommend immediate and active preparations for operations that may be forced upon us by-and-by.' As for the press, it was more or less solidly in favour of sending help. A member of the public suggested that a fund should be collected 'to bribe the tribes to secure the General's personal safety'; a mass meeting was held in Hyde Park; and a clergyman proposed that prayers for Gordon should be offered up in every church in the country. But Mr Gladstone still appeared to have deafness added to all his other shortcomings. Eventually, his readiness to allow Gordon to die was overcome by – not by humanitarian considerations, nor by thoughts of the nation's honour, but by a threat from within his own political party. Lord Hartington, that slow and simple minister of war, had had enough. Unless a relief expedition was dispatched, he proposed to resign.

At about the same time, his fellow peer, the Earl of Selbourne, uttered a similar threat, but his was taken less seriously. The earl was merely the lord chancellor: Lord Hartington, in addition to his responsibility for any wars Her Majesty's government might care to support, was also leader of the Liberal party. If he went, the administration would be split clean down the middle. Human considerations might turn their pleading eyes on him in vain: the queen might talk about the nation's honour; all these were nothing compared to Mr Gladstone's dislike of being dislodged from the seat of power.

He promptly decided that a maximum of £300,000 should be set aside to mount a relief expedition to go to the aid of the beleagured major-general. Lord Wolseley was to take charge of it, which was only reasonable. It was, after all, he who had got Gordon into this mess.

Three hundred thousand pounds is a trifling amount, when one considers what the task involved. Nevertheless, Wolseley was not going to let financial considerations stand in his way. He assembled a force and commissioned a large number of flat-bottomed boats to be built for the expedition. By 9 September, he was in Cairo. By the 28th of that month, he had decided that the quickest route to Khartoum would be by way of the Nile. On that day, the force set off for Wadi Halfa on its first leg of the 1,650-mile journey. Eight days earlier, a messenger had got through to Khartoum with letters bringing news of the proposed rescue operation. They seemed to suggest that help would arrive by early November, and Gordon ordered a 101-gun salute from the city's ramparts. There was little enough to celebrate at the time.

Progress was very slow indeed. Wolseley was a careful, one might say cautious, general, who believed in establishing supply points along the route. At one point, the river makes a large loop, and camels had to be organized for a desert crossing. Well out in front, there was a thirty-five-year-old major named H. H. Kitchener. Like Gordon, he was a Royal Engineer: also like Gordon, he had a talent for reconnaissance. He was in charge of the advanced intelligence service, and responsible for preparing the way. Behind him, a force of about 1,600 troops under the command of General Sir Herbert Stewart was given the task of reaching Metemmah (on the Nile – opposite the Sudan's old capital at Shendi) as quickly as possible. The idea was to concentrate there for the assault on Khartoum, and to link up with Gordon's river steamers. Wolseley also hoped that the sight of his men within territory held by the Dervishes might relieve the pressure on the city. As he was only too well aware, the decision to mount the operation had been taken six months too late. The question, which hovered like a dark shadow over him, was: would his men arrive in time?

The first battle took place at Abu Klea Wells, an oasis in the desert about twenty-three miles from the river. The 19th Hussars, which were out in front, made the first contact. There was, they noticed, a large force of Dervishes ahead of them. Since the news reached Stewart in the late afternoon, he decided that action would have to wait until the following morning. He told his men to bivouac for the night. Shortly after dawn, the troops formed up in a square, hoping that the Dervishes would take the initiative. If they had done so, units positioned out in front would have been able to enfilade the enemy's flanks. But the Mahdi's men hesitated. Stewart gave the orders for the square to advance. Almost simultaneously, the Dervishes came forward and executed a left wheel, which brought them to the rear of the British force. There were about ten thousand of them. A number of naval guns and some of the army's rifles jammed, but it hardly mattered. The two sides were now engaged in murderous hand-to-hand fighting. It was an art at which they were both superlatively good. The British soldier excelled himself when it came to combat with a bayonet, and it was by this kind of encounter that the Mahdi's men had captured their first supplies of fire-arms.

Early in the engagement, the Dervishes broke through the back of the square and penetrated the cavalry formations. But the English infantrymen, although grossly outnumbered, were too good for them. By five o'clock that afternoon, the enemy were in flight pursued by heavy rifle fire. They left behind eight hundred dead. There had, according to a prisoner, been 'an exceptional' number of wounded. Thirty-six British troops were killed and 107 wounded. Among the fatal casualties was Colonel Fred Burnaby of the Royal Horse Guards: the officer who had represented *The Times* when Gordon was in Equatoria. The date was 16 December.

The force moved on to Metemmah, which was captured after another engagement during which General Stewart was mortally wounded. The command now passed to General Sir Charles Wilson, an officer who had made a name for himself in intelligence, but who had little experience of an active command. Like Wolseley, he was cautious. Everything had to be just so, and every detail known, before he would commit himself to action.

At Metemmah, they found the steamers from Khartoum. On one of them, there were the six volumes of Gordon's *Journals*, and three last letters which seemed to be in strange contradiction to one another. One of them reported, very briefly, 'Khartoum all right – could hold out for years.' A note to Colonel Watson, on the other hand, painted a vastly more gloomy picture. 'My Dear Watson,' it began, 'I think the game is up. . . . We may expect a catastrophe in the town in or after ten days.' It was dated 14 December. And, to Augusta, he wrote:

> This may be the last letter you will receive from me, for we are on our last legs, owing to the delay of the expedition. However, God rules all, and as He will rule to His glory and our welfare, His will be done. I fear, owing to circumstances, that my affairs pecuniary are not over bright.

The journals ended with the words: 'NOW MARK THIS, if the Expeditionary Force, and I ask no more than 200 men, does not come in ten days, *the town may fall*; and I have done my best for the honour of our country. Good bye.' The balance, then, seemed to be on the side of despondency, but why that optimistic message about holding out 'for years'? It was probably written in case the steamer was captured: a false clue to deceive the Mahdi. Watson's letter, the final entry in the journals, the note to Augusta – they had all been dated the 14th. Everything suggested that he expected the situation to worsen considerably on or about Christmas Day. It was now 19 January. Were they too late? One might have expected Wilson to make a desperate dash up river to Khartoum and to hell with prudence. But the meticulous intelligence officer would still not take any chances. He spent three days on making reconnaissances, and it was not until the 24th that the force got on the move again. Khartoum was four days' journey away.

15
The Last Encounter

When the *Abbas* steamed away up river with Stewart and Power on board, the walls of solitude closed in on Gordon. There were a number of European consuls left in the city, but he had little time for them. For company, he preferred the sheets of paper which littered his desk, and on which he wrote his *Journals*. They were long, sometimes rambling conversations – mostly with himself. However, he may have intended them for publication, for in each volume he insisted that, if this happened, it should be pruned. Now and then, he broke the pattern of words with a cartoon. Occasionally, he seemed to go beserk with the use of capital letters and copious underlining. Trifling observations would sometimes be interrupted by quotations from the Bible; and one sees this small tired figure, scribbling away frantically into the night, the pile of cigarette ends mounting – the silence broken only by the scratch of his pen and the occasional shot from the ramparts. These journals are the only testimony of life in Khartoum after the departure of the Englishmen. When they were taken upstream in the steamer *Bordein* on 15 December, the supply of information came to an end. Almost everything after that is guesswork.

During the daytime, he would tour the defences, and make frequent visits to the telescope mounted on the palace roof. The soldiers up there were buglers: they were short men, who had to be stood on boxes to be able to fire over the parapets. On one occasion, one of them was knocked over by the recoil of his rifle. 'We thought he was killed by the noise he made in his fall,' Gordon wrote.

Supplies were a perpetual problem. 'Truly I am worn to a shadow with the food question,' he noted; 'it is the continual demand.' Now and then, in his trips around the city, he came across quantities of grain and biscuits that had been hidden away in private houses. Every discovery seemed to extend the period of Khartoum's survival. He introduced a system of rationing for the poor and elderly. In this as in everything, he tried to be scrupulously fair. Sheep and cattle sometimes found their way in from the outside world, but grain was the real need.

He watched himself carefully, with his ego scrupulously monitoring the weaknesses of his id. Other people may have been afraid of his temper, but none more so than he himself. He worked off some of his rage in the comic drawings which adorned the journals – many of them poking fun at Evelyn Baring, who seemed to sum up all that he detested in diplomats. In one of them, Baring – complete with eyeglass and a larger-than-life flower in his buttonhole – is talking to a colleague. The captions read:

Egerton: I can't believe it – it is too dreadful!
Baring: Most serious! is it not? He calls us monkeys! Arrant humbugs!

It relates to the previous paragraph, in which Gordon had observed: 'I must say I hate our diplomats. I think with few exceptions they are arrant humbugs, and I expect they know it.' The drawing, one might say, is for emphasis and relief – as if the thought, having stewed for too long, needed this flourish of a pen to eradicate it. The scars of that unhappy financial assignment in Cairo linger. In a desperate attempt to find a temporary scapegoat for his situation, he takes the commissioners for debt to task, and then the blame slides back on to the statesmen's shoulders. 'We are an honest nation,' he writes, 'but our diplomats are conies, and not *officially* honest.'

His mind turns to food. 'The stomach,' he writes, 'governs the world, and it was the stomach (a despised organ) which caused our misery from the beginning. It is wonderful that the ventral tube of man governs the world, in great and small things.' And yet there are compensations in a diet just sufficient to ward off starvation, and in an unlikable oven of a city thousands of miles from London.

I dwell [he notes in one of his happier moments] on the job of never seeing Great Britain again, with its horrid, wearisome *dinner* parties and miseries. How we can put up with those things passes my imagination! It is a perfect bondage. At those dinner parties we are all in masks, saying what we do not believe, eating and drinking things we do not want and then abusing each other. I would sooner live like a Dervish with the Mahdi, than go out to dinner every night in London. I hope, if any English general comes to Khartoum, he will not ask me to dinner. Why men cannot be friends without bringing their stomachs in, is astounding.

Gordon insisted that the journals should be cut before publication, and it would have been interesting if he had suggested what, precisely, should have been taken out. Without such guidance, an editor could use them as a construction kit from which at least a dozen different portraits could be built. As a soldier, he makes countless plans for the expeditionary force, working out time and again what he would do if he were the commander. Did he blame himself for creating a situation in which it became necessary to dispatch these men? Does he worry about the lives it may cost? Possibly, for he is constantly emphasizing the fact that, as he put it, 'I will not allow that you came for ME. You came for the garrison at Khartoum.' But can he really believe this? Gladstone would have been unlikely to send a powerful body of troops, led by one of the nation's most distinguished generals, to rescue a ramshackle body of soldiers in their struggle against a foe who may have been a terrorist, but was certainly a radical. One doubts whether he ever succeeded in convincing himself on this point.

Of his own feelings, there is no doubt at all. He could have gone on board the *Bordein* with his journals and made his way to safety. There were many other occasions when he could have quit, and left the city to its final agony. But he remained, knowing almost certainly that Wolseley's men would never arrive in time. Gordon, though he would never have admitted it, was an actor, producer and playwright, and the show was the story of his life. There is something almost artificial about these last days: the dispatch of the journals as his final testament, the closing in of fate, the days of unknown mental suffering and, finally (dare one say it?), the Crucifixion. Did it really happen, or was it *contrived*?

Among his many worries was that of reconciling the temporal with the spiritual. One entry reads: 'What a contradiction is life! I hate H.M.G. for their leaving the Sudan after having caused all its troubles; yet I believe our Lord rules heaven and earth, so I ought to hate Him, which I (sincerely) do not.' But there are also more practical things to be considered. So far as he knew, the garrison at Sennar was still holding out. What if the relief force should refuse to go on and save it? Thoughts of resignation whirled around in his mind, but could he afford it? Yes. He can turn to the King of the Belgians, and take up his post in the Congo. 'Therefore,' he concludes, 'I am, so to say, free of Her Majesty's Service.'

On every page, his loneliness shrieks out. It is as if he feels compelled to talk things over with somebody: to think, as it were, aloud. But there is nobody who can understand: only those mute white sheets of paper. He becomes angry again; and then, interested, observes: 'It is very curious, but if I am in a bad temper, which I fear is often the case, my servants will always be at their prayers, and thus religious practices follow the scale of my temper; they are all pagans if all goes well.'

Was his ill-temper a cloak to conceal his fear? Doubtful, for he recognized that he was often afraid. Indeed,

I am always frightened, and very much so. I fear the future of all engagements. It is not fear of death, that is past, thank God; but I fear defeat and its consequences. I do not believe a bit in the calm, unmoved man. I think it is only that he does not show it outwardly.

The years seem to fall away, and Gordon is back in China; praying in the heat and peril of an engagement – not for survival, but uttering a plea that his troops will not run away. Sometimes it seems that he would regard it as a defeat to survive Khartoum: that death, somehow, would be the only possible victory.

He sits at his table, with the thick black silence of the desert beyond, and the hours slide by into the inner recesses of the night. At last, he goes to bed.

> One tumbles at 3.0 a.m. into a troubled sleep [he writes the next day]. A drum beats—tup! tup! tup! It comes into a dream, but after a few moments one becomes more awake, and it reveals to the brain that *one is in Khartoum.* The next query is, where is this tup, tupping going? A hope arises it will die away. No, it goes on, and increases in intensity. The thought strikes me: 'Have they enough ammunition?' (the excuse of bad soldiers). One exerts oneself. At last, it is no use, and up one must get, and go on the roof of the Palace; then telegrams, orders, swearing and cursing goes on till about 9.0 a.m. Men may say what they like about glorious war, but to me it is a horrid nuisance (if it is permitted to say anything is a nuisance which comes on us).

There are only two men at the kernel of this situation: Gordon and the Mahdi. On one occasion, the former receives a rumour that his opponent is travelling a hundred and sixty miles up river to Abba, where he is due to attend the circumcision of his son. 'I hope it is true,' he writes, 'for it will give us ten days' respite. He may also have another dream there, which will tell him not to come to Khartoum, or he may persuade his followers to have one to the same effect. What a comfort!!!' The Mahdi had no such dream: indeed, it is doubtful whether he ever went to Abba. On 10 December, he was sitting down and writing to Gordon:

You have paid no attention to the council and attentions repeatedly sent to you, but have increased in folly; and the numerous kindly admonitions have only made you more haughty and wayward . . . Your letter had reached us in which you deceived the population, saying that British reinforcement is coming to you in three divisions, and that it will soon reach you and give you victory; thus your letter betrays the greatness of your fear, and anxiety, and alarm, as in your deceit you have caught hold of spider-web ropes and have feared to die at our hands. Thou must inevitably die, O thou heathen!

Two days later, there were still 1,796,000 rounds of Remington ammunition in the Khartoum arsenal, 540 rounds of Krupp ammunition, 6,000 rounds for a mountain gun, and sufficient biscuits and grain to hold out a little bit longer. There were just over 8,000 troops left, and two river steamers.

One item in Gordon's journal says, 'I have always felt we [he and the Mahdi] were doomed to come face to face ere the matter was ended.' In life, there does not seem to have been any such encounter – though, on 18 December, it seemed probable. Apparently, the Mahdi sent him a letter, asking whether he could come to Khartoum. Gordon replied that this would be in order, and that he would go over to Omdurman to receive him. He took the precaution of alerting the troops; and taking an escort of four steamers with him across the river. Whether this was a ploy by the Mahdi to capture Gordon, or whether he was dismayed by the gunboats, will never be known. At all events, no meeting took place. The affair turned into a brief battle – after which the Dervishes dispersed, leaving one of Gordon's steamers immobilized by shellfire.

If he had hoped to trick Gordon, it was in keeping with the Prophet's flair for psychological warfare. It may also have been part of a greater stratagem directed at the relief column. Shortly after the battle at Abu Kea Wells, he had sent an envoy to the British, stating that Gordon was now 'wearing the Mahdi's uniform'. The man was also instructed to convey the message that, if the British soldiers adopted the Moslem faith, he would spare their lives. If they refused, they would be slaughtered to a man. He was not taken very seriously.

He was no less ready to deceive his own men. After one engagement, a private soldier in the Duke of Cornwall's Light Infantry came across a saddlebag on a donkey which had been killed four hundred yards behind the captured position. Inside it, there was a note from the Emir General of Berber, stating that Khartoum had fallen on 21 January. It claimed that the Dervishes had taken only fifteen minutes to overcome the city, and that they had 'killed the traitor Gordon', and ended 'Tell your troops'. On 21 January, Gordon was certainly alive – and, so far as anyone could tell, well.

At the battle of Abu Kea, the Dervishes captured a number of British helmets. The Mahdi caused them to be mounted on spears, and paraded round the camp at Omdurman. They were displayed as evidence of his claim to have inflicted a crushing defeat on Stewart's men. Only a few stragglers had survived, he said, and they would soon be accounted for. This theatrical production and its implications was not lost on the men manning the ramparts at Khartoum. Their spirits, already low from lack of food, became even more demoralized. There had been a succession of rumours about the ever imminent relief force which had never arrived. It seemed perfectly reasonable to suppose that it had indeed, been wiped out.

Within the city, there were lesser rumours. One of them had it that the Austrian consul was preparing to go over to the Mahdi with seven female attendants. Gordon hoped he would do so, for he disliked the man. In fact, the consul remained at his post, and was one of those killed in the final massacre. Gordon continued to brood. He worried endlessly about the fate of Stewart and Power. Was he responsible? 'I will own that,' he wrote, 'without reason ... I have never been comfortable since they left. Stewart was a man who did not chew the end, he never thought of danger in prospective; he was not a bit suspicious (while I am made of it).' At the time of writing, this self-accusation was probably true, and he had good enough reason to be. Every day, he was compelled to throw men into prison, and it bothered him.

I hate these arrests [he told a sheet of paper] but one can scarcely doubt so many informants, who declare there was 'trahision' meditated, not from any wish to join Mahdi, but for fear I was not strong enough to hold the city ... I confess I am more perplexed about these arrests than I like; is it a good thing? Or is it not?

But by no means all the enemies were within Khartoum, and nor were they limited to the Mahdi's followers. The British government was as perfidious as the rest of them, and Gordon was in despair. 'Oh! our Government,' he lamented, 'our Government! What has it not to answer for? Not to *me*, but to these poor people. I declare if I thought the town wished the Mahdi, I would give it up.' At about this time, he was worried that the heavy rain would make the mines useless; and as if to add to all his other anxieties, the post office clerks demanded a rise in pay. It was hard to understand, for it was some time since there had been any mail for them to deal with.

The journals presently came to an end, and were sent on their way: six fat volumes in which nearly all of Charles George Gordon lay exposed. When he had seen them off in the *Bordein*, did he begin a seventh volume? He must have done: he must have found some release for the unbearable pressures which were building up inside him. Gordon was at his most articulate on paper. It might even be said that he sometimes talked too much in this manner; but, towards the end, he had every reason to. Food became more and more difficult to come by. People were eating dogs and donkeys and, even, rats The only thing that never seemed to run out was Gordon's supply of cigarettes.

Every day he went to the roof, and studied the landscape to the north through the telescope. Every day, he sought the cloud of dust which would herald the advancing army. Nothing broke the sharp line of the horizon. There had been so

many promises, and so many of them broken, that he went
back to his room in a mood of despondency. He had noticed
recently that the troops and the civilians in the city had
changed their attitudes towards him. Once, he had been the
saviour: the man who would bring comfort and security to
Khartoum. Now, in these last, bitter, days, it seemed that he
had failed them. He had become smeared with the same streak
of treacherous inadequacy that lay behind his comments on
the British government. The soldiers seemed to have lost all
appetite for the war. They remained at their posts, but there
was a listlessness about them which came from fatigue,
hunger and disillusionment. Their reactions were slow: the
fight had gone out of them. Of the two steamboats which had
remained behind after he had sent the rest of the fleet down
river, only the *Ismailia* was now in working order. The other
had been too badly damaged during the abortive expedition
to Omdurman. Gordon could have used it to escape, and he
sometimes considered fleeing to Equatoria. But, after every
conference with himself, he always returned to what he considered to be his duty. These were not just a collection of
Sudanese, with a smattering of Egyptians and Turks: they
were his people. He had to stay with them; and, if Wolseley's
men did not arrive in time, die with them. Amid all this con-
fusion of thought, he never looked sufficiently hard at the
river which ambled sluggishly past the palace wall. The White
Nile was to be the greatest traitor of them all, for the water
was receding as it was apt to do at this time of the year. Mudbanks were becoming exposed, and there were neither mines
nor barbed wire nor any other kind of defence on them.

The 25 January was a Sunday. There had been a great deal
of activity in the Mahdi's camp at Omdurman, and the Dervishes seemed to be massing at the south-western end of the
line. Gordon had remained inside the palace for most of the
day. He was not feeling well. It may have been an attack of
dysentery, or possibly the liver complaint from which he had
been suffering. Had he toured the defences, he would have

noticed that the telegraph wires, which connected them with the palace, were out of order. He would also have observed that many of the men were deserting. Traffic across the Nile was particularly heavy that day.

In the evening, he ordered a spectacle designed to mislead the Mahdi. There was a tremendous display of fireworks and the band played for several hours. The Mahdi was unimpressed, and went on with his work of sending men across the river in preparation for an attack. Nor did this sudden pretence of a gala atmosphere do anything to revive the flagging spirits of the troops. Those who remained at their posts waited with the resignation of men utterly worn out. Eventually, the final rocket swam into the sky, and the band put away its instruments. Khartoum went quietly to sleep.

The attack began shortly after dawn. According to one report, a citizen named Farag Pasha went around the perimeter beforehand, opening all the gates. But this was later denied by a number of competent witnesses, and the fact that Farag Pasha was executed three days later in the market place at Omdurman, seems to support their statements. Another account suggests that 'a pasha' (unnamed) marched all the troops to the far side of the city, telling them that an attack was expected from this quarter. In fact, the Dervishes were planning to break in through the positions which were now empty. What is certain is that the Mahdi's generals had a thorough knowledge of Khartoum's defences. They knew them to be weak on the side facing the river: a portion of the parapet had tumbled down, and it was easy to reach this sector by running over the newly exposed mudbanks. This is where the initial break-in occurred – though Farag Pasha probably did open one of the gates as an act of surrender. With such a strong force of Dervishes already in the city, he realized that any further combat was useless.

Throughout their painfully brief struggle, the Khartoum troops put up a poor defence, and the Dervish casualties amounted to only eighty to a hundred men. Many of the soldiers laid down their arms as soon as they saw the enemy approaching. The Egyptian warriors were slaughtered on the spot. The Sudanese were ordered to march off to a prison camp at Omdurman, where they were stripped of everything they had. Within the city, the sound and fury were of insane dimensions. These were not professional soldiers executing a carefully devised plan: they were an ill-disciplined swarm of fanatics who had been enticed by the Mahdi's magic. Now their minds were inflamed by the prospect of murder, rape and plunder. Their first objective was the palace, for that was where Gordon would be, and that was where the spoils of war would be greatest.

The classical ending to the story of Charles George Gordon is that he was awakened by the shooting at 3.30 a.m. He went on to the roof to see what was happening, and then he went to his quarters in the west wing to get dressed. He put on a white uniform with all his decorations pinned to it; girded on his sword and picked up a revolver. At some point he sent a message to the engineer of the *Ismailia*, telling him to raise steam. Perhaps this suggested that he intended to make a last-minute attempt to escape, but the engineer was too afraid to leave his home. He is then reputed to have walked to a flight of stairs leading to the council chamber. The palace servants down in the basement had already been murdered, and the Dervish ringleaders were at the foot of the staircase. 'Where is your master the Mahdi?' Gordon is said to have asked. Less than a second later, the first spear was plunged into his body.

On the other hand, this was not the account which reached England when, a fortnight later, the first news of the fall of Khartoum was received. According to this report, Gordon, one of his aides, and twenty men, were seen marching from the palace to the church at the Austrian consulate. As they came into the open space at the front of the building, a party of Dervishes fired at them. Gordon fell instantly, and only one or two of the men managed to scramble to cover. Shortly afterwards, the Austrian consul was murdered in his house. The Greek representative and a doctor were both taken prisoner.

Once the fighting was over, the Dervishes went out of their minds in a rampage of lust and vengeance. During the next six hours, they slaughtered more than four thousand people; and then, at about ten o'clock that morning, the Mahdi sent orders that enough was enough, and the killing must stop. The looting, however, continued – though it turned out to be disappointing. As an incentive to take the city, their leaders had promised the men as much gold and silver as they could carry. They searched for it in vain. All they could find was a mass of Gordon's now useless paper money.

According to custom, the casualties were decapitated. Gordon was no exception. His head was taken in triumph to the camp at Omdurman, and shown to the rebel leader. The prophecy had come true: he and the Mahdi were at last face to face.

What did the living eyes expect to see in the face of the dead? The mask of a great warrior? Gordon had relinquished that role a long time ago. There had been no battle of Khartoum: the city expired from exhaustion. When the Dervishes entered it, they scrambled over what was, to all intents and purposes, a corpse. Gordon may, as people said, have died a hero's death, but who was this man? The substance had travelled north in that chaotic jumble of thoughts and contradictions which appeared in the *Journals*. Only the shadow remained.

The Mahdi is said to have been angry when he heard about Gordon's death, but this was probably a pretence. He caused his head to be displayed on a tree, where passersby threw stones at it. In any case, as Kitchener wrote,

There is little doubt, in my opinion, that, had he (the Mahdi) expressed the wish, Gordon would not have been killed. The presence of Gordon as a prisoner in his camp would have been a source of great danger to the Mahdi, for the black troops from Kordofan and Khartoum all loved and venerated Gordon ... The want of discipline in the Mahdi's camp made it dangerous for him to keep as a prisoner a man whom all the blacks liked better than himself, and in favour of whom, on a revulsion of feeling, a successful revolt might take place in his own camp.

A steamer carrying General Wilson reached Khartoum two days after the city had fallen. The vessel was driven back by heavy fire, but Wilson and his officers noticed that no flags were flying from the palace, and there seemed to have been a great deal of destruction. The only news of Gordon's fate came from Arabs on the river banks, who were unanimous in their opinion that he had been killed. It was not until thirteen years later that the Dervish revolt was crushed at the Battle of Omdurman, and Khartoum was retaken – with, on this occasion, Kitchener in command of the British force. But the Mahdi did not live to be defeated. He died six months after Gordon, and a mystery surrounds his death. According to Major F. R. Wingate in his book *Mahdism and the Egyptian Sudan*:

> a woman, daughter of a townsman who had lost children, wives, property, and all, in the long siege [of Khartoum], submitted to outrage. On the night of the 14th June she gave the effeminate and debauched prophet a deadly poison and after lingering in great agony he died on the 22nd of the month.

On the other hand, Rudolf C. Slatin Pasha, a former governor of Darfur who was one of the Mahdi's captives, said in *Fire and Sword in the Sudan* that he died of typhus. 'Gathering up all his strength,' Slatin Pasha wrote, 'with one final effort, he repeated a few times the Mohammedan creed, crossed his hands over his chest, stretched out his limbs, and passed away.'

Whichever the true reason, Gordon had been avenged – though this was probably the last thing he would have wanted.

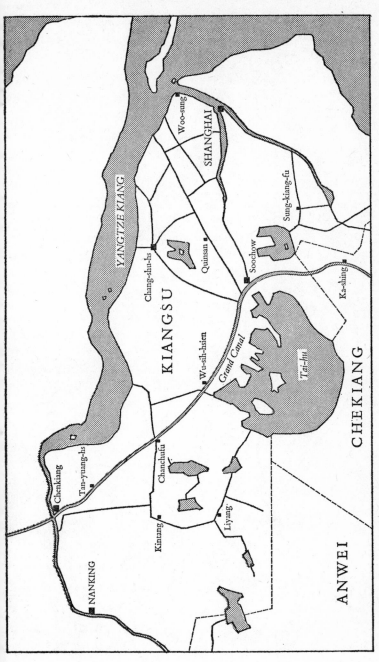

China: Shanghai and environs

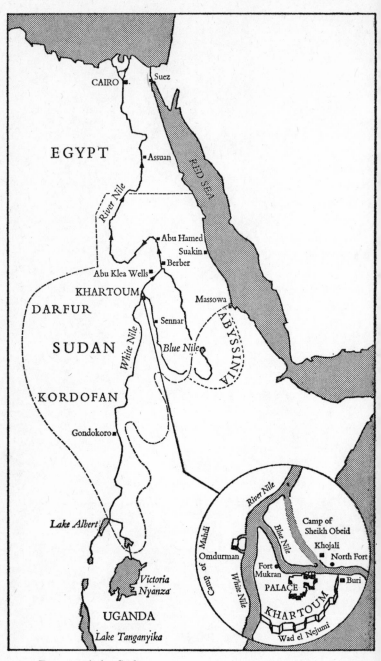

Egypt and the Sudan

Bibliography

Barnes, The Rev. R. H., and Brown, C. E., *Charles George Gordon: A Sketch* (London, 1885)

Beresford, Lord Charles, *The Memoirs of Lord Charles Beresford* (London, 1914)

Boulger, D. C., *The Life of Gordon* (London, 1891)

Elton, G. E., First Baron, *General Gordon* (London, 1954)

Gordon, Charles George, *Colonel Gordon in Central Africa, 1874-9* (London, 1884)

Gordon, Charles George, *Letters of General C. G. Gordon to his Sister M. A. Gordon* (London, 1888)

Gordon, Charles George, *General Gordon's Khartoum Journal* (London, 1885; 1961 edition by Lord Elton)

Gordon, Henry W., *Events in the Life of C. G. Gordon* (London, 1886)

Nutting, Anthony, *Gordon; Martyr and Misfit* (London, 1966)

Robertson Scott, J. W., *The Life and Death of a Newspaper* (the story of the *Pall Mall Gazette* – London, 1952)

Slatin, Sir R., *Fire and Sword in the Sudan* (London, 1896)

Strachey, Lytton, *Eminent Victorians* (London, 1918)

Turner, E. S. *Gallant Gentlemen – A Portrait of the British officer, 1600-1956* (London, 1956)

Wilson, A., *The Ever Victorious Army* (London, 1868)

Wingate, Sir R., *Mahdism and the Sudan* (London, 1891)

Wortham, H. E., *Gordon – An Intimate Portrait* (London, 1933)

Index

236

237